T0357343

What's a Christian, Anyway?

Finding Our Way in an Age
of Confusion and Corruption

GLENN PACKIAM

NELSON
BOOKS

An Imprint of Thomas Nelson

What's a Christian, Anyway?

Copyright © 2025 by Glenn Packiam

Published in Nashville, Tennessee, by Nelson Books, an imprint of Thomas Nelson. Nelson Books and Thomas Nelson are registered trademarks of HarperCollins Christian Publishing, Inc.

Published in association with The Bindery Agency, www.TheBinderyAgency.com.

Thomas Nelson titles may be purchased in bulk for educational, business, fundraising, or sales promotional use. For information, please email SpecialMarkets@ ThomasNelson.com.

Unless otherwise noted, Scripture quotations are taken from the Common English Bible. Copyright © 2011 Common English Bible.

Scripture quotations marked ESV are taken from the ESV® Bible (The Holy Bible, English Standard Version®). Copyright © 2001 by Crossway, a publishing ministry of Good News Publishers. All rights reserved.

Scripture quotations marked NIV are taken from the Holy Bible, New International Version®, NIV®. Copyright © 1973, 1978, 1984, 2011 by Biblica, Inc.® Used by permission of Zondervan. All rights reserved worldwide. www.zondervan.com. The "NIV" and "New International Version" are trademarks registered in the United States Patent and Trademark Office by Biblica, Inc.®

Scripture quotations marked NKJV are taken from the New King James Version®. Copyright © 1982 by Thomas Nelson. Used by permission. All rights reserved.

Any internet addresses, phone numbers, or company or product information printed in this book are offered as a resource and are not intended in any way to be or to imply an endorsement by Thomas Nelson, nor does Thomas Nelson vouch for the existence, content, or services of these sites, phone numbers, companies, or products beyond the life of this book.

Names and details have been changed in many of the author's stories to protect privacy.

ISBN 978-1-4002-4830-8 (TP)
ISBN 978-1-4002-4831-5 (audiobook)
ISBN 978-1-4002-4827-8 (ePub)

Library of Congress Cataloging-in-Publication Data on File

Printed in the United States of America

24 25 26 27 28 LBC 5 4 3 2 1

For the people of Rockharbor Church—
Keep believing and living like it's true (because it is).

NICENE CREED

We believe in one God,
the Father, the Almighty
maker of heaven and earth,
of all that is, seen and unseen.
We believe in one Lord, Jesus Christ,
the only Son of God,
eternally begotten of the Father,
God from God, Light from Light,
true God from true God,
begotten, not made,
of one Being with the Father.
Through him all things were made.
For us men and for our salvation
he came down from heaven:
by the power of the Holy Spirit
he became incarnate from the Virgin Mary, and was made man.
For our sake he was crucified under Pontius Pilate;
he suffered death and was buried.
On the third day he rose again
in accordance with the Scriptures;
he ascended into heaven
and is seated at the right hand of the Father.
He will come again in glory to judge the living and the dead,
and his kingdom will have no end.
We believe in the Holy Spirit, the Lord, the giver of Life,
who proceeds from the Father and the Son.
With the Father and the Son he is worshipped and glorified.
He has spoken through the Prophets.
We believe in one holy catholic and apostolic Church.
We acknowledge one baptism for the forgiveness of sins.
We look for the resurrection of the dead,
and the life of the world to come. Amen.

(1975 ECUMENICAL)

Contents

Author's Note

This book began as a sermon series, first preached at my previous congregation in Colorado Springs ten years ago. But the seeds were planted in worship six years before that when we began confessing the Nicene Creed regularly at our evangelical, charismatic megachurch. I saw people on the edge of deconstruction glimmer with hope as they began to discover a faith bigger than the tainted American church they knew. They were being invited into a mystery that transcended the tidy certainty they had grown up with. When we finally did a sermon series on the Nicene Creed, expounding on the meaning of each phrase and connecting them to the words of Scripture they were built on, it became clear that this ancient confession of Christian faith had something to say to the church today.

When we moved to California three years ago, I revisited the series, rewriting each sermon for a new context and a new cultural moment. Retrieving the wisdom of an old creed for a people known for innovation and forward thinking seemed counterintuitive. But their response was surprising. Through dozens of conversations—in the lobby and hallways, in my office and in coffee shops all over Orange County—I heard how fresh this vision of God and of the Christian life was. People were struck by the beauty and simplicity of it all. And even more than that, they found it profoundly helpful in cutting through the fog to return to the heart of what it means to truly be a Christian.

As I've traveled around the United States and other parts of the world, speaking to pastors and church leaders in a variety of different contexts, I heard stories of how difficult it has been to help people sort through the things that matter and the things that don't. Followers of Jesus are struggling to know what things are essential to our faith and what things are peripheral—or worse, are distortions and corruptions. The scandals and abuses of church leaders have only heaped pain on their confusion. These conversations confirmed my own pastoral experience of walking with the disappointed and disillusioned, the disoriented and disrupted. "Tell me about the faith you've left," I want to say. "Chances are, it was not Christianity anyway."

Through it all, the fire for this project began to burn hotter. We need help finding our way. We need to know what it means to be a Christian.

I offer this backdrop for two reasons: first, to provide a bit of a peek into the origins of this book; and secondly, to offer my gratitude. To the people I have the privilege of serving as pastor—and to all in previous seasons—I am profoundly grateful to be a witness to God at work in your lives and to be allowed to join in that work in some small way. To the pastors and church leaders who have opened up to me and become fellow travelers on the road to resilience in ministry and personal health, I count it a privilege to be numbered among you. May God continue to grant us the grace to love well and lead faithfully those whom God has entrusted to our care.

Ultimately, this book has come from the church, and it is written *for* the church. I have labored over these words in the hope that we would be, in Lesslie Newbigin's words, the "hermeneutic of the gospel"—*a way for everyone to know that Jesus is good news for the world.*

Foreword

There was once a time when GPS satellite navigation didn't exist, and people had to rely on massive, fold-out paper maps to navigate. My wife says she loved those giant, physical maps because she could see the full picture of where she was going—the entire journey laid out in front of her. Now, imagine with me for a moment; you and your family are returning home from an epic road trip. You're driving through the back roads of the Appalachian Mountains. It's dark. Road signs are covered by trees. Then your digital navigation goes out! Panic sets in as you realize you don't have one of those big old maps! You are mapless. You drive, hoping to find the right direction or someone to help. But all you find is that you are lost in the back country of the Appalachian Mountains. Your gas tank is nearing empty. You want nothing more than to get home, but without a map, you're stuck, confused, and dazed.

That disorientation is where many followers of Jesus find themselves in the twenty-first-century American church. Nothing seems simple or easy. People are negatively deconstructing their faith or abandoning Jesus outright. Shallow discipleship plagues the church, sapping the life out of her. A consumer-driven approach to faith has left many believers unchanged and powerless. And *where do we go from here?* is the question many of us are asking as we wander in the dark in exhausting circles, unable to find our way home. It feels a little like we lost our map.

But I have some good news. In *What's a Christian, Anyway?* my friend Glenn provides us with an ancient map that will lead us home. This book is about the Nicene Creed, a time-tested guide back to the heart of the Christian faith. This ancient statement of belief shows us the way to Christ-exalting, "cruciform" life, which is the life you and I were created to experience. The gospel of King Jesus is the royal announcement that Israel's Messiah has defeated sin and death, overthrowing the powers of evil through His sinless life, sacrificial death on the cross, and His resurrection. And all who call on His beautiful name are forgiven, declared righteous, sealed by the promised Holy Spirit, and eternally united to Jesus as a covenant member of His body, the church (1 Cor. 12:12, 27).

God has united you with Christ Jesus. For our benefit

God made Him to be wisdom itself. Christ made us right with God, He made us pure and holy, and He freed us from sin. Therefore, as the Scriptures say, "If you want to boast, boast only about the Lord" (1 Cor. 1:30–31 NLT).

Glenn, like an expert map reader, will help you find the way to your Father's house. First, you will learn that the abundant life you were created to live is found in knowing and loving the source of life, the Father, the Son, and the Holy Spirit (John 10:10).

Second, his love for the church will captivate you and spur you on to love the church and see your place in it. Glenn rightly points out that we Christians in the West tend to think individualistically, while the biblical faith is communal just as God is a triune community of co-equal, co-eternal persons. Individual salvation only exists so God can grow the global, multiethnic family that he promised Abraham long ago (Gen. 12:1–3; Gal. 3:8). Jesus, the "seed of Abraham," brings this blood-bought, Holy Spirit–birthed, Father-loved family into being (Gal. 3:16, 26–29). This family is born into peace by Christ (Eph. 2:14–16) and unified in the Spirit (Eph. 4:1–6), and has equal access to the Father (Eph. 2:18–20). "This is our vocation, our calling," Glenn reminds us.

Third, he loves God's people. On every page you will sense his love for you, the reader. As I read the book, I can see how hard Glenn fought for you to understand. He is clear, compelling, and Christ-exalting. This book is a devotional for your heart and a training manual to equip God's people for the work of ministry and for mission with Jesus.

We do not have to be lost wanderers anymore.
We have a map that leads home.

Dr. Derwin L. Gray

Cofounder and lead pastor of
Transformation Church

Author of *Lit Up with Love:
Becoming Good-News People to
a Gospel-Starved World*

CHAPTER 1

Finding Our Way Home

I 'm lost. It shouldn't worry me this much—I'm not in the woods, or in a jungle, or up in the mountains, or in the desert. I am driving in the suburbs. But it's dark outside, and I have no bearings, no clue where I am. So I'm a little worried.

To be fair, this is a pretty normal occurrence for me. I have a notoriously bad sense of direction. But in my defense, we moved here not more than six months ago. I am still learning the streets and neighborhoods and freeways.

And as those close to me know, I usually rely on maps on my phone, even to tell me how to get to places that I should absolutely know how to get to on my own. But tonight, my phone won't stop freezing. I try resetting it a couple of times. But every time it turns back on, it freezes again with the screen showing half of one app and half of another. So I set aside my malfunctioning phone and do what any normal person would do when they find themselves lost and afraid: I pray. I pray like a plane crash survivor in an Amazonian jungle. *Lord, help me.*

I drive slowly toward an intersection, vaguely confident that I should turn left. I do. It seems to get more familiar. Then I am unsure. *No need to panic.* Still, my heart is beating more quickly. The family is out of town, back in Colorado for a visit. Here I am in a beautiful neighborhood in Southern California as the hour creeps toward midnight, unable to find my way home.

Suddenly my phone awakens from its spell, casting out the demons that seized its operating system. Apple Maps opens. The address registers. A route appears.

I am saved.

Mildly lost at night on the streets of a small city is surely no crisis. But something primal reflexively signals the alarm in our bodies when we can't get home. Home is where we are oriented toward. Home is where we must go. And if our path is impeded, by peril or by sheer directionally challenged dumbness, we start to feel the tremors of danger.

Home is where safety is.

Darkness is not a time for delay.

When night falls, it is time to go home.

GOING HOME

I heard a lecture once where the speaker argued that all great stories are about *home*. A person leaves home to go on an adventure. Or a person struggles to make his way back home. Or maybe a person fights to defend her home. Yes, *The Iliad* and *The Odyssey* are such stories, but so is the Bible. God creates a home for Himself and for His creatures. Humans decide to try to run the home themselves, becoming a threat. God exiles them and they must find their way back home. They can't, so God comes after them and brings them back home to Himself. More than that: God remakes the world and makes His home with humans after all. "So that God may be all in all" (1 Cor. 15:28 NIV).

Jesus told the human story as a story of two sons who leave home. One leaves to go on a self-indulgent adventure, seeking short-term pleasure around every corner; after that brother returns, the other leaves because his home is no longer conforming to his desired norms of acceptable behavior. The first stumbles on his way home, ready to accept a lower status within it; the other refuses to return home even when his status is preserved by the father.

Our own story is bound up with our home. Far as we may go, we long to return.

Within the macro stories of Scripture and the human heart, there are smaller stories, smaller journeys away from home or journeys of return that mark the moments of human history, and even church history. We mark whole eras with words like *exile* or *captivity* to describe a departure that the church has made or ground that may have been lost or situations and stability that may have shifted. A word like *exile* makes sense only because *home* makes sense. Exile is not home. *This* is not *that*. Conversely, we use words like *renewal* or *revival* or *return* to describe a homecoming of sorts—either ours to God or God's to us. Some Christian traditions speak of a *visitation* of God, implying that God has come to make His home where He belongs: with His people. We sing a poignant phrase like "I'm coming back to the heart of worship" to indicate our own wandering and homecoming.[1]

Home is where we belong. Home is when all is right and well. And every time we cannot find our way home, like me on that mid-February night, our pulse starts to quicken.

The church in Western societies today seems to have lost its way. Faithful Christians feel it in their bones. As a pastor, I hear their questions and listen to their laments frequently. *What is going on with Christianity?* Surveys confirm my experience. Barna Group's research has found that about half of US Christians today describe present-day Christianity negatively, using phrases like "hypocritical" and "out of touch with reality." Pastors are declining in credibility, with only about a third (34 percent) of US adults saying that they would consider a pastor or a priest as a trustworthy source of wisdom on spirituality.[2] Even those who don't call themselves Christians know something is amiss. We hear various descriptors and qualifiers thrown about: *It's the evangelicals! It's the right wing. It's the left wing. It's white Christians. It's progressive Christians. It's American Christians. It's the Reformed Christians. It's the charismatics.*

But these labels are less helpful than we may imagine. We are prone to tend to the speck in another tradition's eye while remaining blind to the plank in our own. Surely it is better to simply say it the way confessions are meant to be prayed: *We have sinned. Like wandering sheep, we have lost our way.*

Good Shepherd, come lead us back home.

JENGA AND THE LOSS OF FAITH

"Losing our way" is only one way of putting it. Losing our faith, or the ability to believe, is another. When we say it like that, it is more serious, more urgent, more dire. And for many, it most certainly is. The headline is not just about the church losing her way; it is about people who have lost their faith.

When we lose our ability to believe something, it's either because the content of belief is no longer *plausible* or because the carrier is no longer *credible*. To put it another way, when we believe, we are asking two questions: Is the statement *plausible*? And is the source *credible*? In the 1960s, sociologists Peter Berger and Thomas Luckmann came up with the term "plausibility structure" to describe the scaffolding that sets the norms for what is considered believable. It is a subconcious framework for shaping how individuals perceive reality and interpret the world around them.

Let's try an example of a plausibility structure with a non-faith-related scenario. If a news headline says that electric cars are outselling gas-operated cars, a plausibility structure made up of the awareness of increased production of electric cars, efforts to reduce carbon emissions, and advances in battery technology makes the headline plausible even if it is surprising. *Yeah, I can see that*, you think to yourself. The statement is plausible in today's world because there is a scaffolding around it. That would not have been the case fifty years ago.

I propose that there are also "credibility structures"—networks of relationships or sets of experiences that make a statement credible because of the people who believe it. If a plausibility structure is about a statement being possible, a credibility structure is about a source being reliable. A credibility structure has to do with trustworthiness.

Let's try an example of a credibility structure. If a friend tells you that Taylor Swift is secretly recording again, and your friend is connected to a network of Swifties who are in the know, and you have a long personal relationship of trust and reliability with your friend and know her to be an honest and intelligent person, you are likely to believe her—and the Swifties she's connected to. The scaffolding of relationship and experience is the credibility structure around her and her claim.

All belief relies on scaffolding. But not all scaffolding is reliable.

Think of a tower of Jenga blocks. Each plank represents people or events or details of your story or context that have made faith plausible—your parents loved each other and created a loving home, and they taught you about the love of God in Christ Jesus; your friends found an anchor during turbulent teen years by reading their Bibles and going to youth events; your church created a community of people in similar life stages or with similar challenges who helped each other recognize the work of the Holy Spirit in daily life.

But then your parents get a divorce; your friend deconverts; your pastor has an affair. One Jenga block after another gets pulled from the stack. And soon, the tower of faith comes tumbling down. Faith feels harder and harder to maintain. It all seems less plausible. That is the impact of plausibility structures.

Barna's research affirms this trend. Among those who were raised Christian and have left the faith (which is the story of about 12 percent of US adults today), seven in ten say things like "I have simply let go of the core religious beliefs I held as a child," "My childhood faith has not helped me as an adult," and "I have a hard time trusting religious institutions."[3]

In America—and certainly in other parts of the world too—Christians are finding it harder to believe not simply because the content of faith is no longer plausible; but also *because the credibility structures have failed.* The statements of faith are hard enough to accept; the source of these statements—the church—is getting more difficult to trust. Scandals have rocked the Christian world from the Catholic Church to the megachurch, from Anglican priests to celebrity pastors. Christians have allowed themselves to be co-opted by political parties and social movements. Bible verses have been clumsily thrown into cultural conversations with little attention to nuance or context.

Down goes another Jenga block.

Not only has Christianity become less *plausible* for the individual, but the parallel and overlapping reality is that Christians have become less *credible*.

Over the past few years, I, along with many others, have made the observation that *opposition* toward Christianity has tapered off into *indifference* toward Christianity. After 9-11, many were talking about how religion in general and Christianity in particular were beginning to be seen as irrelevant at best, dangerous at worst. But militant atheism gave way to indifferent agnosticism. *Christianity? Buddhism? Religion? Spirituality? Who knows what's true? Who cares?*

But we're beginning to see another shift. Indifference is shifting into outright distaste. It's not militant atheism or indifferent agnosticism, but rather dismissive cynicism. Not *who cares*, but rather *who needs this?*

Unlike the decline of credibility that Christians faced in recent decades, this loss of credibility is not because Christianity has been found wanting on logical or intellectual grounds. Christianity is losing credibility in the West because it has broken relational trust and fractured social bonds. Our world has less of an intellectual problem with faith and more of an emotional one.

But let me stop right here and clarify: I don't mean that pejoratively. So often, people speak of emotions as though they are the lower or animal-like part of a human; as if the mind and its thoughts are lofty, but the heart and its feelings are fluffy, unserious, or unsubstantial.

I don't think of emotions that way. Human beings operate on the gut level far more than we'd care to admit. As New York University social psychologist Jonathan Haidt has persuasively argued, we are not rational beings first, but feeling beings who rationalize our intuitions.[4] Or, if that bothers you, consider how Ashley Null, the leading living scholar on Thomas Cranmer, the great English Reformer, summed up Cranmer's view of human beings: "What the heart loves, the will chooses and the mind justifies."[5]

So what we love, what we find desirable, matters.

Is it possible that today, the world around us finds Christianity unbelievable mostly because they find it undesirable?

A DIFFERENT HERMENEUTIC

We don't need better *apologetics*, though I'm all for those. Christians in every age need to articulate the reasons for belief in their own way for their own day. We need a different kind of *hermeneutic*—a different way of making sense of the claims that Christians make. Commenting on the changes he was noticing in Britain in a post–World War II reality, Lesslie Newbigin, the missionary bishop to India, said as much. It's a long quote, so let's take it a few lines at a time.

I have come to feel that the primary reality of which we have to take account in seeking for a Christian impact on public life is the Christian congregation.[6]

This is his central claim. It is the church who makes the gospel believable, the community of Christians who make Christianity credible.

How is it possible that the gospel should be credible, that people should come to believe that the power which has the last word in human affairs is represented by a man hanging on a cross?

I am suggesting that the only answer, the only hermeneutic of the gospel, is a congregation of men and women who believe it and live by it.[7]

Newbigin is not diminishing the many other ways Christians engage in public life or live out the nature of the gospel as a "public truth"—an announcement and a reality that affects everybody, everywhere. He lists examples like "evangelistic campaigns, distribution of Bibles and Christian literature, conferences, and even books such as this one." But he argues that "these are all secondary, and that they have power to accomplish their purpose only as they are rooted in and lead back to a believing community."[8]

The believing community is the credibility structure that makes the gospel believable. Women and men who, by the grace of God and the power of the Holy Spirit, "believe it and live by it" make the good news believable. Christians—in the fullest sense of the word—make Christianity credible.

TYING A ROPE TO THE BARN

There's an episode of *Little House on the Prairie* where a blizzard arrives around Christmas. Pa mentions to his friend that they better put the "rope about to the barn." Now, I grew up in Malaysia, just outside the capital city of Kuala Lumpur. I don't know the first thing about barns or blizzards. But my father-in-law is a farmer in rural Iowa. A second-generation farmer, the son of a man who spent hard-earned money to acquire land and worked that land with horses in the early twentieth century, my father-in-law retained not only the ethic of the previous generation but also the romance of manual work. He resists GPS tractors and Roundup Ready beans. He wants to be around the cattle and the dirt himself.

The barn outside their house is worn down, the wood aged and brittle. It stands a mere fifty yards from the house. And yet, as my father-in-law explains, blizzards in the Midwest can get so brutal that even a short distance, traveled with frequency and familiarity, can be hazardous. The wind and snow can be blinding and disorienting, and a short jaunt to the barn to close it up can result in hours of wandering out in the cold. You need a rope between the house and the barn to keep you walking straight, to keep you from straying off in the blinding blizzard, to save you when stumbling on snow drifts. You need a rope between the house and the barn just to make it home.

And so it is with us.

Christians have lost credibility because we have lost our way. We have given lip service to the formula of faith, but ignored the life it was meant to produce. We have our doctrines sorted, but our love is disordered. The result is a lived Christianity that falls short of the living faith of the church at its best.

The church has also lost credibility because it has mishandled power. Barna Group found that only 18 percent of non-Christians say Christians are good at listening to others' stories and standing up against wrongdoings and injustice. Instead, about a third of non-Christians agree strongly that Christians "see themselves as better than others" (34 percent).[9] We have raised our voices for the wrong things and at the wrong times. We have taken a stand when we should have taken a knee in prayer and in service. We have tried to rise up when we should have taken up our cross in sacrificial love. We believe in Jesus, but our lives look nothing like Him. This is not the kind of "believing community" Newbigin had in mind. This is not the kind of church that makes the gospel credible.

There is no shortcut to regaining credibility. There is no PR campaign or ad blitz that can cure what ails us. What we need is not a better reputation. What we need is a return to the core of who we are called to be. We need to come home.

We need a rope—a rope to hang on to, to guide us, to remind us where it all began. Maybe in years past the weather was clearer; maybe there was less confusion. But now, in a swirl of cultural opposition and conflicting Christian opinions, we are blind and cold and in danger of getting lost.

How are we to find our way? Amid the flurry of opinions broadcasted on X (formerly Twitter), arguments expounded on blogs, winsome talks aired on podcasts, how are we to distinguish between *popularity* and *credibility*?

Our age is not unlike the early decades of the fourth century. Christianity had been multiplying rapidly for three hundred years with the number of Christians burgeoning from roughly a thousand to multiple millions. It grew beyond the margins as powerful people and influential teachers began to convert to Christianity. Yet popularity was not always accompanied by credibility. While many churches kept the apostles' teachings, some had been mixing it with pagan superstitions and philosophy. Traveling teachers were twisting core tenets of the faith, causing confusion. On top of that, as wealthy and powerful people became Christians, the Way of Jesus was at risk of corruption. These early Christian communities needed a rope to keep them tethered to Jesus and His kingdom; they needed a reminder of the Way.

The threat of false teaching was present even in the New Testament era, as the letters of the apostles reveal. A simple summary of the heart of the Christian faith was essential. A compact, single-sentence version of this is in 1 Corinthians 15:3–4: "Christ died for our sins in line with the scriptures, he was buried, and he rose on the third day in line with the scriptures."

But more needed to be said. In the century after the New Testament era, a few Christian teachers developed an outline of the faith that every follower of Jesus could trace. In the early AD 300s, a council of more than three hundred church leaders gathered to settle disputes and to affirm the teaching of the apostles. What emerged was a robust "rule of faith."

The Council of Nicaea codified the core Christian confession and confirmed the letters and books that counted as Christian Scripture. Both creed and canon came from this monumental gathering. Though the Creed was expanded slightly and refined at a later gathering in Constantinople in AD 381, it is still referred to as the Nicene Creed and is affirmed and confessed in worship by Protestants, Catholics, and Orthodox Christians all over the world. Because of its historical and global significance—and for the sake of brevity—we will simply refer to it as the Creed.

In the chapters that follow, we're going to walk line by line through the words of the Creed, one of the oldest confessions of Christian faith. As we unpack each line, we will explore what it means to be a Christian. But we won't stop there. We're going to examine what it means to believe these words and what it looks like to live like we believe these words. By the time we get to the end of this book, it will be clear that a definition is not the goal. Faith is not an end in itself; faith must work itself out in love (Gal. 5:6). We are not simply on a quest for truth. We are finding our *way*—the way of Jesus and His kingdom.

And for that, we're going to need a rope to lead us home.

CHAPTER 2

What's in the Bag?

S everal years ago when our two older kids were going through kindergarten, each of them in turn played a game called What's in the Bag? Each child in the class would take turns bringing in a brown paper bag with a secret item in it, and the first letter of the item written on the outside of the bag. The child would also write a simple poem, giving clues for the hidden item. For one of our kids, we put something in the bag and wrote the letter O on the outside. The clue was straightforward prose: "It's a color and a food." One classmate shouted, "An Oreo!" To his great disappointment, it was, of course, an orange.

What's in the Bag? is sort of like the game people play when trying to answer the question of what it means to be a Christian. The clues vary, sometimes from church to church, because the contents of the bag seem to change as people keep adding stuff.

Oh, to be a Christian, you need to vote with the conservative party or the progressive party.

And you can't watch those kinds of movies or TV shows.

And you may not want to put your kids in public school.

You've got to put God first and then country—that is, America.

You've got to embrace freedom of all kinds—but especially as it relates to guns and markets.

Cultural values, behavioral norms, personal preferences, and more get lumped in with Father, Son, and Holy Spirit until no one is quite sure what really is in the bag.

And so people don't know what they are saying yes to.

They like some of what's in the bag, but they've been told it's a package deal. Take it all—the holy doctrine and the human dogma, the beautiful gospel and the obnoxious behaviors—or nothing.

And so, they opt for nothing. They walk away. Keep your bag, they say. Like the rich young ruler, they walk away sad, but not because of anything Jesus said and not because they were unwilling to surrender their whole lives to the true King, but because they can't say yes to the bag they've been given. The Christianity they have been invited into is untenable and undesirable. You see, it isn't just that culture has shifted or that not many are asking the question to which we claim to have the answer; it's that Christians have lost their way. We no longer know what lies at the center of our faith.

What's in the bag? It's anyone's guess.

IS IT CHRISTIANITY?

In the early 2000s, a sociologist named Christian Smith conducted a survey of America's religious youth. He found teenagers who self-identified as believing in God and having a faith of some kind. He then asked follow-up questions to see what they actually believed about this God. The survey addressed the distinction between what British theologian Helen Cameron called "operant theology" and "espoused theology." Operant theology is the implicit theology by which people live, the set of values and convictions about God that guide their decisions and shape their perspectives, even if those values and convictions are unarticulated or subconscious.

Smith found that the operant theology of young people who claimed to be Christians was a far cry from Christianity. In fact, it was so unlike Christianity that he needed a new name for it. He came up with the phrase *moralistic therapeutic deism*.[1]

Moralistic because God is concerned, above all else, with how I behave, and whether I'm following His arbitrary code. Don't be naughty; be nice. Don't smoke, don't chew, don't hang out with those who do, and so on.

Therapeutic because God really wants me to feel good about myself and about my life. Yes, He has rules and stuff, but in the end, He just wants me to have a good time and for things to go well for me. God is a way for me to feel better about life.

Deism because this God doesn't really get too personal. He is detached, distant, and for the most part, uninvolved.

In short, the young Christians that Smith surveyed believed in a God who is far away, who wants us to do good, and who wants us to feel good.

A few years ago, when I wrote *The Resilient Pastor*, many Christians were becoming aware of a new corruption to the Christian faith, a version of Christian nationalism that insisted God was responsible for America's history, central to America's identity, and invested in America's destiny. Some have, over the years, referred to this tendency as a kind of civil religion—a public version of ideology and morality that loosely connects to Jesus or relies on Jesus-y language but really serves as bonds of solidarity for society. (One possible root for the word *religion* is literally the things that bind or tie us together.) Jesus is confessed for the sake of unifying or preserving or reclaiming "America," itself a reference to more than a geopolitical nation-state and more broadly to an idea or an ideal.

Initially, much ink was spilled on how Christians have ruined politics by this pursuit. Subsequent analysis has questioned whether people who hold this view may actually be confessional Christians—*What is their creed or belief?*—or practicing Christians—*Do they participate in the life of a local church?* But the outcome is that the name of Christ has been slandered to the wider world.

While the church has drifted into problematic expressions of Christianity like moral therapeutic deism and Christian nationalism, the wider culture has become more individualistic. And that's an important part of understanding Christianity's credibility problem today. In trying to describe the landscape of a post-Christendom world, I have used the metaphor of a shift in tectonic plates, resulting in a surge of oceanic waters that has left us with a messy aftermath. As the connection between Christianity and culture became more tenuous, the rise of alternate meaning-making systems of spirituality created a culture awash with confusing and conflicting values and beliefs. But if there were a way to distill the overlapping qualities of the dominant way of seeing the world, I would propose we call it something like *individualistic syncretistic pluralism.*

Sociologist Jean Twenge, who has studied the trademarks and tendencies of all six living generations from the "Silents" to the "Polars" or Gen Alpha, reports that "Millennials are the least religious generation of younger adults in American history." It remains a possibility that Gen Z will surpass millennials in their abandonment of organized religion. But why is it that religion is on the decline among millennials? Twenge's answer: "In short, because it is not compatible with individualism—and individualism is Millennials' core value above all else. Individualism promotes focusing on the self and finding your own way, and religion by definition promotes focusing on things larger than the self and following certain rules."[2]

CREDO

The word *credible* is related to the word *creed*. Both are about belief. To be credible is to be believable. To have a creed is to have something to believe in. What I am proposing here is that the church's original confession of belief is what can help us become believable.

As Newbigin said, it is a church that believes and lives the gospel that makes the gospel believable. If the Nicene Creed is the rope that leads us home and reminds us who we are and if being who we are called to be makes the gospel believable to the world, then we might say it like this: believing and living the Creed can make a Christian credible. It keeps us from adding things to the bag. It is a purifier, an irreducible minimum of the Christian faith.

But this creed is much more than that. It is meant to hold our feet to the fire, to lift our heads up higher, reminding us how life-altering this kind of faith really ought to be. Creed and credibility are related because when Christians return to the essence of our faith, we reclaim its power. That doesn't mean culture and structures don't matter or that we can live a kind of decontextualized version of Christianity. No, that's not possible. The Word became flesh, and faith in the Word is always enfleshed again and again in real human beings and real human communities. The church will look and feel different all around the world. But the Creed reminds us of the core and invites us to live from it.

The Nicene Creed is a rule of faith. Maybe you've heard

of a "rule of life," a pattern of spiritual disciplines that helps us to be with Jesus and to become like Him. A rule of faith is an essential complementary component of Christian discipleship. If a rule of life helps us to keep company with Jesus in the course of daily life, a rule of faith keeps us on the path; it keeps us close to the heart of our faith. The Creed functions in at least three ways. Let's name them and try a few metaphors.

First, it is an *outline of theology.* The Creed was an early, official, robust outline of apostolic faith. I know, I know . . . some of you might protest that theology is not the answer. You're thinking, *Maybe* you *care about such things, but I don't care about theology. Who needs theology? I just love Jesus, and He loves me.* There is something truly beautiful about that heart. It is childlike and simple and gets the very core of the gospel: being loved by God and loving Him in return. We ought never to lose that heart, never to lose the simplicity of childlike faith.

And yet, we are to grow to a mature faith. For our bodies to grow, we need proper nutrition. If someone were to prepare a nutritious meal for you—let's say, salmon with black pepper, spinach, and tomatoes—you would benefit from it, even if you did not know why. You don't need to be a nutritionist to benefit from a nutritious meal. But if you want to learn to cook for yourself and develop a habit of healthy eating and healthy living, you have to learn a few principles of nutrition.

Theology is a bit like that. Good theology—from authors or preachers or podcast pontificators—can nourish your faith without you understanding why. But if you want to begin to grow and feed yourself, you have to learn a little bit about what makes a particular theology good or bad, robust or anemic. Our faith cannot grow on the theological equivalent of a Happy Meal.

All of us have a theology; the only question is whether it's a good one or a bad one. Everybody has a way of thinking about God. That's what Christian Smith's survey of America's youth showed. Everybody has a view of God, a way of thinking about Him, and a way of understanding how He thinks about us. The question is, are we thinking rightly or, to be more precise, thinking Christianly or not? That's what the Creed helps us grapple with.

When children learn to write, they don't start with an empty page. They usually begin by tracing their letters over dotted lines. Over and over again, they trace a letter. One whole line of the letter *A*; one whole line of *B*. Soon, they can write those letters without the guidance of the dotted lines.

That's the idea of a pattern of faith. You trace these words until you know them by heart. Until they find a way inside your core, until your vision of God is Father, Son, and Holy Spirit; until your picture of love is Christ who came down "for us and for our salvation"; until your ultimate hope is "the resurrection of the dead, and the life of the world to come."

If the Nicene Creed were only an outline of Christian theology, you might be tempted to put this book down. Save it for another day when you want to study or stretch your brain. The truth is, the Creed is so much more.

It is also an *instrument of unity*. The Creed is sharp enough to exclude, yet strong enough to unify. Phrases in the Creed are clear enough to mark the difference between those who are Christians and those who aren't.

The sharpness of the Creed and the distinction it creates should not alarm us. It is not intended to make us hostile or belligerent toward others. It isn't a means for us to elevate ourselves above "outsiders" and look down our noses at them. None of us deserves the grace that has been given to us. The church, those who have believed this news and received this gift, exists in the world for the sake of the world, not to stand over or escape from the world. But for the church to be given "for the life of the world," as Orthodox theologian Alexander Schmemann put it, the church must stand apart from the world in some sense.

Schmemann wrote that Christian worship—the liturgy—begins as a "real separation from the world."[3] Having ascended in worship and having been "immersed in the new life of the Kingdom," Christians are able to return to the world with faces reflecting the "light, the 'joy and peace' of that Kingdom" and to be its true witnesses.[4] The separation from the world is the first liturgical act; the sending back into the world is its last.

But for the church to be given for the life of the world, the world must also be able to see where we stand together. As noted earlier, the Creed is sharp enough to exclude, but it is also strong enough to unify. The church is like a wagon wheel. The spokes of the wheel are like the different streams of the body of Christ. The more you follow the spokes away from the center, the farther they get from one another. Every stream of the body of Christ has a special perspective or emphasis. Most of the time, these unique angles are gifts to the wider church.

My family is a microcosm of this. My mum was raised Anglican, and for many years, when my sister and I were young, we attended an Anglican church. The beauty of the prayer book and the awe of participating in the liturgy—the standing and kneeling, the candles and the incense—provoked a reverence that I remain grateful for. When faith for my parents became something they began to fully surrender to, they had the experience of becoming "born again," of allowing Jesus to become Lord and Savior of their lives. A friend invited them to join a Bible study led by a Baptist pastor, where a love for the Word of God was instilled in them.

Later, in separate experiences, both my dad and my mum came to know the presence and power of the Holy Spirit filling their lives in notable ways. Eventually, our family began attending a Pentecostal church. The passion for the lost and the conviction that God would meet us personally and powerfully in prayer and in worship left an indelible mark on our lives.

And so it is that each stream of the church brings different gifts to the wider body of Christ. Our various emphases can be good, but a point of distinction can easily become a point of division. The more we focus on how different we are, the farther we get from one another.

But the more we follow the spokes toward the center,

the closer they get to one another. When the church moves toward our shared center, our unity gains visibility. And what is at the center? What unites us? What can we all hold on to? The Creed reminds us: It is the Father, the Son, and the Holy Spirit. That's why the Creed can be an instrument of unity.

Finally, the Creed is a *guide in uncertainty*. I have only hiked one "fourteener" in my whole life (a "fourteener" is what mountain people call a mountain whose peak is 14,000 feet or more above sea level). I did it the summer that I moved to Colorado, mostly because I didn't know any better. A group of people was about to hike Pikes Peak, and I decided to go along. I mean, how hard could it be? Well, let me tell you! The trail itself is about thirteen miles, but the change of elevation that occurs over those thirteen miles is the killer. You gain over 7,500 feet in elevation with about 3,000 feet of that gained in the first three miles! All in all, it took me about seven and a half hours.

I was grateful to have been accompanied by a large group from our church. One nice guy carried my backpack for me, and another guy sat with me when I needed a break every thirty minutes during the final three miles of the climb. But you know what really made it possible? Not just that others were going with me, but that others had gone before me. I was not the first person on the Barr Trail to Pikes Peak, and I'm glad I wasn't! There was a trail, a well-maintained and clearly marked trail because many others had done this before. Someone had cleared away the thicket and brush and trod down the weeds. Someone had laid markers and built a camp about two-thirds of the way up. There are even websites with pictures and advice for a successful ascent.

The Creed is like a trail. Someone has walked this path, they have marked the pitfalls, cleared away the obstructions, and even set up a camp at a strategic place. The early fathers fought through errors, cut down heresies, and made a clear path for how to think and talk about and pray to the Father, the Son, and the Holy Spirit. The stanzas about Jesus are longer—sort of like Barr Camp on the trail to Pikes Peak—helping us stop and reflect more deeply, keeping us from critical mistakes about the Son of God.

Many of the phrases in the Creed are included precisely to avoid specific heresies and to keep Christians on the only path to the summit. Yes, we have to walk the trail for ourselves; but no, we need not walk it by ourselves. And, bless God, there is a trail!

CREDIBLE FAITH

The next ten chapters will take the lines of the Nicene Creed and help us do more than understand them. The goal is not mere theological formation, though that is of some benefit. My hope is to encounter the God the Creed reveals and, in doing so, discover who He calls us—indeed empowers us—to be as we are immersed in His life.

The Creed is organized in three "articles" or sections—one

for each person of the Trinity. The section on Jesus is appropriately the longest because, as the early Christians knew, if you get Jesus wrong, the whole thing falls apart. Tucked into the section on the Holy Spirit are some pretty powerful lines about the church, about the forgiveness of sins, and about the hope of bodily resurrection.

With that in mind, here's how we're going to map out our journey. We'll take a chapter to examine the weight of the first three words of the Creed, words that get repeated in each of the three sections. Then we'll spend one chapter on the first Person of the Trinity—the source of everything. After that, we'll take three chapters to talk about Jesus. Next, we will spend a chapter on the Life-Giver, the Holy Spirit. In the next chapter, we'll talk about the church—yeah, I know, a really complicated topic. Then we'll unpack baptism and forgiveness and how revolutionary the good news is meant to be. And finally, we will lift our eyes to the horizon of hope, further than what we're used to seeing—beyond heaven.

But credibility is not just about the right confession. All along the way, we will ask what it would look like to really live like we believe these things. So in the last chapter of the book, we'll pull some of those threads together and sketch out a vision of a life that says "Amen" to the words of faith. We will take seriously what the apostle Paul wrote: "The greatest of these is love" (1 Cor. 13:13). The list he was referring to was faith, hope, and love. Having covered faith and hope, we'll hear the divine invitation to a life of love. For the Christian, the proof of *right belief* is supposed to be *true love*.

What's a Christian, Anyway?

Each of the three articles—actually, the songwriter in me prefers to think of them as "stanzas"—begins with the same three words. Like a good hymn, the Creed opens with a repeated refrain: "We believe in . . ." It's those three words that we go to next.

CHAPTER 3

All Together Now

We believe in . . .

My father was raised as a Hindu. He became a Christian as he was dating my mother. His family cut off relationship with him after his conversion, refusing to attend the wedding since it was held in a church. In fact, there was quite a bit of turbulence surrounding the whole season from my dad's conversion to their wedding because his father passed away suddenly from a heart attack. Some of my dad's siblings blamed him for causing stress that led to their father's death.

Over the years, family dynamics with my dad's side of the family slowly improved. Visits with my uncles and aunties on my dad's side eventually became cordial. As devout Hindus, my aunties had the red dot on their foreheads, a symbol of inner piety. And in their homes were pictures of various Hindu gods on display, sometimes even in a small room dedicated as a shrine of sorts. As my parents kept reaching out in love and hospitality, the relationships kept growing. In fact, several of my dad's siblings and in-laws actually came to faith in Jesus before the end of their lives.

There are some beautiful threads of redemption in the story. But I share parts of it here to say that growing up, I had no concept of religion as private or individual. Religion in Asia—indeed, in many parts of the world—is public and communal. Changing religions was a family affair with generational implications. It was not, as it is in many Western countries, a matter of private opinion or personal choice.

In our context in the West, we think that being public about faith necessarily entails being obnoxious or controversial. That is, of course, often the case. Everyone knows the two subjects to avoid around the holiday family table are religion and politics. But Malaysia is a salad bowl of ancient religions with Muslims, Buddhists, Hindus, and Christians living relatively peacefully among one another. On my street as a kid, there were homes with Buddhist altars beside the front door, burning incense sticks. There were portraits of Hindu gods like Ganesh that adorned living rooms and dining rooms. And there was a mosque at the end of the street, blasting daily prayers through a loudspeaker for the neighborhood to hear. Christians, who make up about 10 to 12 percent of the population, were the quiet bunch by comparison.

But there was nothing private about religion.

I emphasize this to help jolt us out of our modern notion that faith ought to be a private matter, that belief—both what people believe and how deeply they believe it—should be a matter of preference or personality. This notion of a private faith is so prevalent that the Barna Group found in their recent study that 56 percent of US Christians believe their spiritual life is entirely private. We have assumptions that we overlay onto our thinking about Christianity that have more to do with our cultural context than with the nature of faith in general and the Christian faith in particular.

In his fascinating book *The Christians as the Romans Saw Them*, early church historian Robert Louis Wilken finds various ways of showing how the Romans struggled to classify what "Christians" were. They didn't quite fit into their category of "religion," because religion for the Romans referred to regional rituals that bound a people together. But Christians claimed to be a "new kind of family" that united people of various ethnicities and territories. This was not a group of people united by a common soil or blood.

Pliny, a Roman governor in the early second century, described Christians as a "club," a kind of social group, perhaps to imply that they might have seditious intentions or political claims.[1] He was right about their political claims— Christians confessed Jesus as "Lord," using the very word that Roman propaganda used of Caesar. But Pliny knew he was wrong about describing them as a club because these people were not all from the same social stratum. Why would free persons willingly associate with slaves? How could men and women mingle together without it being sexual or scandalous? Rumors began to fly. And the Romans kept scratching their heads.

And then there was the Christian preoccupation with the *Way*—a commitment to living according to a different set of values and principles. There was a clear ethic they sought to adhere to. The closest thing to compare Christians to in this regard was a *schola*—a school of philosophy. There were indeed many elements of Christianity that were like a philosophy. There were teachers and there were students or disciples. But there was also worship. Pliny wrote that Christians gathered early in the morning, singing hymns to Christ as if to a god.

So what were these Christians? A religion, a club, or a school? A mystery indeed. One thing they were never accused of being: private or individual.

"I KNOW THAT . . ." VS. "WE BELIEVE IN . . ."

The three stanzas of the Creed open with the same three words. Three words that shape three sections. "We believe in . . ." I suspect that if somehow the council of early Christian church leaders had convened in an American city in the last fifty years, they might have chosen a different set of three words to open each stanza. Instead of *We believe in . . .*, it might have been *I know that . . .*

I because the individual is primary—even though no one stands on their own, we espouse the myth of individuality. *Know* because we have fallen in love with the myth of certainty, even if the thing we are certain about is "my truth." *That* because the only kind of knowing we trust is the knowing that comes from a distance—the myth of objectivity.

If we were to write a confession today, it would be grounded in three foundational modern myths—the myths of individuality, certainty, and objectivity—and it would open with the words *I know that.* It's worth asking what grounds the words that actually open each stanza of the Nicene Creed: *We believe in . . .*

We roots us in community—for faith is only possible together. *Believe* reminds us that we are encountering a great mystery beyond our normal modes of knowing. *In* invites us to proximity, for God does not desire to be an object but a subject—not a thing to be known from a distance but Someone to be known personally.

Now contrast these presuppositions—these foundational paradigms:

Community over individuality.
Mystery over certainty.
Proximity over objectivity.

We're beginning to see that the Creed is not a cold doctrinal statement. It is a vibrant call to worship. Let's break down the significance of each of these first three words.

What's a Christian, Anyway?

"WE . . ."

The first word of the Nicene Creed is a word of plurality. Now, before some folks come after me, I am aware that some versions in prayer books use *I*. I am likewise aware that the Apostles' Creed uses the singular first person and is no less holy for it. I get it. It's just that I think the *We* here is significant for us. In the Nicene Creed's original Greek, the first word is the first-person plural form of the word for *believe*, which translates to "We believe."

One of the unintended consequences of emphasizing personal faith over the past few decades of evangelicalism has been the mistaken notion that faith is *individual*. We want people to come to a place where they have faith *for* themselves, but we've let them cross over into thinking they can have faith *by* themselves.

Dozens of people I've talked with over coffee or a meal or in my home or in my office have told me they're not sure if they can be a Christian anymore. When I ask them to share more, it usually relates to one or two doctrinal items they carry significant doubt about: *Did the virgin birth actually occur? Is the resurrection literal? Is there really a final judgment?* And so on. Often, they are still compelled by Jesus. And the idea of God coming to forgive our sins and redeem the world seems too beautiful to completely dismiss. But there are some lines that they struggle to get themselves to say, metaphorically speaking.

It's almost as if we've been trained to imagine faith like

a one-person kayak. When we struggle to row the oars of faith, we conclude that we should get out of the boat. After all, the boat is not going to advance itself. If you can't row, you shouldn't be in the boat.

But faith for the Christian is much more like a rowing crew. I see them out in the Back Bay here at Newport Beach. With each person rowing in sync, the large boat glides smoothly across the water. If one person were to stop rowing, the boat would still keep moving. (Someone who knows this sport far better than I do will want to say that the whole point of crew is rowing together and in sync! So for a better metaphor, think of an old galley ship from the Roman era where hundreds of people row to keep it moving.)

Analogies aside, the point is, followers of Jesus are in one large boat together. (Please resist the urge to make a dad joke about *fellow-ship*.) If you're struggling with faith and need to set your oar down, that's fine for a season. Just stay in the boat. Don't jump overboard. Faith is not a solo sport. Let others row when you cannot.

If you're wrestling with something about the boat, it's okay: Stay in the boat. If you can't affirm every line, it's okay: That's why we say it together. And that's why we say "We." When your faith is weak, another's is strong, and when your faith is strong, someone else's will be weak. And together we lift one another. That is the power of *We* in the "We believe" of faith.

I heard a story of a guy who crosses his fingers behind his back when he says the lines in the Creed about the virgin birth. Some may scorn such behavior. But I think, *Isn't it marvelous that he's gathering with the church, confessing with the church, praying with the church?*

Jesus knows that our faith will waver. Just as He said to Peter, so He says to us: "I am praying for you" (Luke 22:32). Perhaps that is the most powerful *I* in the communal *We*: Jesus, the first among many brothers and sisters, joins us in prayer and worship. Indeed, we are joining Him because we are in Him.

So whether you're doubting or deconstructing or struggling or wavering, *stay in the boat*. Keep gathering with the church. Let the faith of others carry you for a season. Let them sing for you, pray for you, believe for you. Stay in the community of faith. In time, your oar will hit the waters again.

"... BELIEVE ..."

Every once in a while it hits me that I now live a mere twenty minutes from Disneyland. *Disneyland*. The Happiest Place on Earth. The place where dreams come true. I was eight years old when my parents took my sister and me to Disneyland. It was the trip of a lifetime. Flights for a family of four from Malaysia were not cheap, and the journey across the Pacific took well over twenty hours. And now, here we are, twenty *minutes* away. All that to say, we've been to Disneyland a few times now.

The moment of arrival is magic. All the anticipation and wonder, all the joy and energy. It lasts for the first few rides, but then as the lines get longer and the day gets warmer, the magic begins to fade. Moods change. Food prices enrage. And it becomes clear that it's time to go.

But if there's one word that captures the gospel according to Disney, it's *believe*. Believe in yourself. Believe in your dreams. Believe in the impossible. For the most part, it's innocent and even inspiring. But it's not an entirely helpful association with the notion of belief.

Belief, for our cultural context, is *make-belief*—a kind of fiction we accept for the effect it has on us. Religion falls into this category. "You can believe in anything that helps you make it through life," a person might say. "So long as it isn't harmful to others," they might quickly add, "your belief is your belief." Belief is private, personal, and above all irrelevant to me. It is, after all, *your* belief.

I was describing an experience I had in a time of prayer to a friend of mine who has no religious beliefs, and his response to me was something like "I'm so glad that was helpful for you." For this friend—and for much of our culture today—religious belief is not gauged by its relation to truth or reality. Rather, belief is judged by its *usefulness*. When it comes to belief systems, the question is no longer "Is it true?" but "Is it helpful?" In fact, the Barna Group has found this in their research of non-Christians time and time again. Barna often asks, "What might bring you into a church?" or "What would help you consider exploring the Christian faith?" The top answers from non-Christians are essentially that they would come or consider it if it would help them improve their lives.

What's a Christian, Anyway?

The *privatization* of belief combined with the *functionalization* of belief results in a *relegation* of belief to the sidelines. If this is just what *you* believe and if belief systems are just ways of making it through this lonely life, then belief is abstract. It's an idea or a set of ideas that is useful—nothing more, nothing less. Belief, understood this way, demands nothing of you. If it remains useful, you keep it. If it fails to be helpful, you abandon it.

Early Christians had a very different understanding of belief. More on that in a minute.

There is one other twist on belief. For some, it is the Disney-fied notion of belief that leads them to actually reject all forms of belief. "It is much better to stick with what we can *know*," they might say. Certainty is better than fantasy. Who needs to wish upon a star when you can hustle and make your goals happen? Thus, instead of the word *believe*, our current creed would say, "I know . . ."

But faith, as Christians have understood it, is neither fantasy nor certainty. It is, instead, an invitation into a great mystery. It points us beyond ourselves. The object of our belief is not ourselves, as if faith were a way of turning inward, like the plug on an extension cord plugging into its other end. The object of our faith is not our dreams, for those are wishes and ungrounded hopes. The object of our faith is a Person, a great triune Being. As theologian Darrell Johnson wrote, "At the center of the universe is a Relationship."[2]

Faith is a way of bowing low before the mystery of this relationship. It is a humbling of ourselves before the Creator, the Redeemer, and the Sustainer—the Father, Son, and Holy Spirit. When we say, "We *believe*," we are saying that we cannot know, for knowing implies grasping fully, and knowledge of God can never be exhausted.

Yet it does not mean that we are making this up. *Believe* for the Christian signifies a reality greater than us and a revelation that comes before us. In the Bible it is God who speaks first. Not a creature or a human. God is a speaking God, a self-revealing God, a God who delights in disclosing Himself to us so that we might know Him—indeed, so that we might *believe* in Him.

The early church planter Paul wrote that even though he himself had received a dramatic vision of the risen Jesus, belief for him was what had been handed down to him. "I passed on to you as most important what I also received: Christ died for our sins in line with the scriptures" (1 Cor. 15:3). Belief for the Christian is always *received*. What we receive—from the church, from the first followers of Jesus, through the Scriptures, from God Himself—is what we believe.

Rather than wishful thinking of fantasy or the prideful illusion of certainty, faith is a humble entrance into mystery.

"...IN..."

Faith, to say it again, is neither fantasy nor certainty. It is, instead, about mystery. But not just mystery. Not mystery in the kind of vague ambiguity of a generic "pray to the universe" kind of spirituality. No, there is mystery to the Christian faith because we are drawing near to the triune God. Distance is what allows for both fantasy and certainty. Think of all the crazy ideas people had about the moon or stars or space in general. It wasn't until the age of powerful telescopes and actual space exploration that our understanding gained complexity. Distance allows us to reduce things to simplistic half-truths that are easy to feel sure about. But nearness is humbling. Come closer to the glacier, and you will feel the grandeur of its size. Get out into the dark ocean, and you will know that its depths are beyond our reach.

Faith for the Christian is marked by mystery because faith is about *proximity*.

The object of faith is not an idea but a Person. And our relationship to the object of our faith is meant to be intimate. If we can say that at the center of the universe is a relationship, then at the center of our faith is the invitation to join in relationship with this God. We do not have to stay far away. We were not made to stay far away. We were made for relationship—not just relationship with each other but with God. That's why Paul was fond of describing Christians as the ones who are "*in* Christ."

There is a world of difference between saying, "We believe *that* . . ." and "We believe *in* . . ." To illustrate the difference, let me tell you about my favorite French acrobat, a man named Jean François Gravelet, who performed feats of tightrope walking in the mid-1800s under the stage name Charles Blondin. On the morning of June 30, 1859, twenty-five thousand people gathered with a sense of anticipation—and perhaps a touch of morbid curiosity—to watch Blondin attempt to walk across a tightrope over Niagara Falls. Both banks of the falls teemed with a multitude of spectators from all strata of society to see what kind of history would be made that day.

The online *Smithsonian* magazine records that "children clung to their mothers' legs; women peeked from behind their parasols. Several onlookers fainted."[3] When he got about a third of the way across, Blondin stopped, sat down on the cable, and called for the *Maid of the Mist*, the tourist boat, to anchor beneath him. He threw down a line, hauled up a bottle of wine, drank it, and started off again, "breaking into a run after he passed the sagging center."[4] Wild. He made it safely to the other side, and after a twenty-minute rest, he walked back, this time with a camera in tow.

The *New York Times* called it a "reckless and aimless exposure of life," while Mark Twain referred to Blondin as an "adventurous ass." Nevertheless, over the course of four decades, Blondin crossed over Niagara Falls on a tightrope more than three hundred times.[5]

On one of his most famous trips across, on August 14, 1859, he carried his manager, Harry Colcord, on his back. Blondin is recorded instructing his manager as they began their walk over the rushing falls: "Look up, Harry . . . you are no longer Colcord, you are Blondin. Until I clear this place be a part of me, mind, body, and soul. If I sway, sway with me. Do not attempt to do any balancing yourself. If you do we will both go to our death."[6]

This, I think, is what faith in God is like. "We believe *that*" is a statement *about* something; it is what is known as "propositional truth." There is some distance between you and the thing you are proposing. In a mythologized version of Colcord's crossing on Blondin's back, Blondin asked for volunteers from among the crowd. The people who cheered for him might have said they believed *that* Blondin could cross Niagara. But only the one who got on his back believed *in* Blondin.

Faith is more than cheering from the banks of the falls. Faith is not believing *that* there is a God. Faith beckons you onto the wire, not to walk alone or to balance yourself but to cling to Jesus.

HOLD THESE WORDS

As we begin our journey through the lines of this ancient confession of faith, hold these words in your heart and mind. *We believe in . . .*

Don't approach these lines as cold, hard facts. We are not here to merely attempt to understand doctrine. What we're after—what the Lord wants for us—is to meet the God this Creed confesses. Words are signifiers. They are signs that point to something. In this case, these words point to the truest and greatest reality: the relationship at the center of all that is. Father, Son, and Holy Spirit. We do not come to feed our minds alone but to awaken our hearts.

To say these words is to pray. We confess the Creed as a way of drawing near, of entering into the reality of who God is. And we are to be changed in the process. The goal, remember, is not simply to believe but to live like we believe. This is what makes us truly credible Christians.

So come. Let us come together humbly into the mystery, drawing near to God, clinging to Him as we read and pray:

We believe in . . .

CHAPTER 4

The One and Only

We believe in one God,
the Father, the Almighty
maker of heaven and earth,
of all that is, seen and unseen.

When the actor Leonard Nimoy was given the line "Live long and prosper" as his character's signature phrase, he knew the perfect hand gesture to accompany it. Growing up in an Orthodox Jewish synagogue, he had seen the rabbi repeatedly hold up his hand with the fourth and fifth fingers touching each other, the second and third fingers touching each other, and the thumb spread apart.[1] It was a *W*, the shape of the Hebrew letter *shem*—the first letter of the word *shema,* which is the first word of the great charge and blessing: "Hear, O Israel: The Lᴏʀᴅ our God, the Lᴏʀᴅ is one" (Deut. 6:4 ɴɪᴠ).

I'm not sure how many die-hard Trekkies would know the biblical connection in the show's most famous sign. There is something marvelously profound, even if it wasn't entirely intentional, about linking the ancient Jewish Shema to Mr. Spock's blessing to "live long and prosper." The fusion of the words of Moses with the words "where no one has gone before" brings together the ancient and the future, the tradition and the unknown, in an implicit claim: *A flourishing life is the result of knowing and acknowledging the source of life.*

"The Lᴏʀᴅ our God, the Lᴏʀᴅ is one." Hear this—really hear this—and you will live, truly live.

SINGULARITY AND SUFFICIENCY

The early Christians, of course, had no clue how the Shema would figure into twentieth-century American pop culture, but they knew it was the bedrock of faith. So when it came to finding the opening words for the Christian confession of faith, it may have seemed an obvious choice. Go back to how it all began, to the very earliest confession of the people of God: the Lord is *one.*

The claim that God is one may not ring with power for us, but that's because in Western cultures that have been reshaped by atheism and agnosticism, the debate is not about which of the gods is the true god, but rather if there is a God at all.

But in the ancient world, there were all sorts of gods, and half gods, and humans who could become gods, and gods who gave up their divinity, and on and on it went. And so the question was not whether there *was* a god, but rather *which* god and what he or she was like.

It was into this world of polytheism and superstition that the Israelites, beginning with Abraham, began to claim with confidence that there was *one* God who was above all other gods. And *this* God was Israel's God—the God of Abraham, Isaac, and Jacob. That's why the Shema opens by saying, "The LORD, *our* God . . ." The God of Israel is the one, and the one God above all gods is Israel's God.

Against the claims of people around them who said you needed one god for rain, and another god for crops, and another god for fertility, and yet another god for victory in battle, the family of Abraham said, "No. There is only one God you need. He is enough." The "enough-ness" of God is, in fact, one of the meanings that scholars suggest is behind the name El Shaddai. This God, *our* God, He is the only one you'll ever need.

The early Christians underscored that, preserving the Hebrew Testament's revelation of God by opening the Creed with the words "We believe in one God . . ." Somehow this one God exists in three Persons, but we must not be confused about what we cannot understand: This God is *one*. The only one.

The *singularity* of God points to the *sufficiency* of God.

MORE THAN ENOUGH

What would it look like to live like it's true that God is sufficient? Imagine living like God is the only god you need. We talk a lot about idolatry in our churches, but what *is* idolatry?

Idolatry is treating something that is not God as if it is. It is asking something *finite* to give you something *ultimate*. It is believing in the *temporal* in order to gain the *eternal*. It's staking your life on a promise that cannot be kept.

Idolatry can also work the other way: making God into our own image or into the image of something we can control. This was the sin of worshiping the golden calf in the wilderness. The people of Israel took their jewelry and fashioned a creature they understood, a creature that perhaps they had seen venerated in Egypt. And they said of it, "This is the God who brought you out of Egypt." They made YHWH into something they could get their hands on, something they could shape and control.

So idolatry is treating something that is not God as if it is God; and idolatry is treating God like something that is not God.

Let's think a bit more about how we fall into both kinds of idolatry. Whenever we say, "Well, I'm so glad Jesus saved my soul and forgave my sins and secured my eternal destiny, but when it comes to how I make money, I've got to just play hardball or be cutthroat or do what works in the real world," we are essentially saying, "Jesus is Lord of my afterlife, but the market is lord of my work life." That's not all that different from the multi-god world of ancient Israel's neighbors. We make the market into another god, a thing we give allegiance to, a god whose laws we follow and adhere to.

Or take another example: a friendship or a relationship. One of God's great gifts is companionship, whether in marriage or in deep friendships. But human companions are still finite; they are creatures. As such, there are limits to how well or how deeply or how consistently they might love us. But when we make a human relationship the ultimate center, we are asking a person to be for us what only God can be for us.

Now, let's think about the second kind of idolatry. When we craft a Jesus who agrees with our politics or ethics, we are at risk of making God into something He is not. Such a god may be more palatable, more reasonable, or even more relatable. But it is not the God revealed in the Scriptures and in Jesus.

You can see how easily we start to live like God is not enough. We live like we believe that we need other things, other people, to function with just as much power or significance in our lives; we live like we need to be God's handlers and interpreters, shaping and reshaping Him for our context. These are the things that erode the believability of our faith. A person outside the faith may wonder, *If Christians believe God is enough, why do they keep clamoring for the levers of worldly power?*

To live like God is enough does not mean we live meager and joyless lives, stripped of all that is good and beautiful in the world. In fact, that's what the very next words in the Creed's opening lines address.

SOURCE AND SUPREMACY

"We believe in one God, the Father, the Almighty . . ."

Right here is where I might lose some of you. Why "Father"? What about mothers? Is this the pseudo-religious root of patriarchy?

Hold on. Stay with me. The Scriptures—and indeed, the Creed—use the word *Father* for a host of reasons, but gender is not one of them. The word is not a statement about the so-called maleness of God. Rather, *Father* is about naming God as the Author and Originator.

But we also refer to the first Person of the Trinity as "Father" because He is the Father of our Lord Jesus Christ. And when Jesus taught us to pray, He taught us to address God as He does, to name Him as *our* Father too. We are not, of course, the "eternally begotten of the Father" (and we will come to that phrase in a later chapter), but we are the adopted children of God. We are not confessing a faith in a distant deity. We are not listing attributes or checking off a list of character qualities. We are approaching the one with whom we have been set in relationship, the one we now call Father.

Even so, this kind of naming is tricky for many of us. We

tend to start with our earthly fathers and then work our way upward to God. But may I suggest, hard as it might be, we start instead with Jesus? Who is the God revealed in Jesus? Jesus said, "Whoever has seen me has seen the Father" (John 14:9). What kind of God do you see in Jesus? Now turn your eyes with Jesus upward to the one He called Father. What was Jesus' relationship like with this Father? How did Jesus talk to Him? What did Jesus say about Him?

Remember that famous story Jesus told about a father who pulled up his robe and ran in an undignified fashion to hug and kiss his wayward child to welcome him home? That is getting us closer to the picture. If we concentrate on Jesus long enough and pay attention to how He revealed the Father, we need not think of our earthly fathers at all. I understand that what I'm describing here is the journey of a lifetime for many people, so please be patient with yourself. But in your journey, let's not cast aside the naming of the first person of the Trinity.

The word *father* is paired quickly, almost like the poetic technique of parallelism, with the word *almighty*. *Almighty* brings out another note—like a harmonic resonance of a musical note—from the word *father*: It makes us think of the *supremacy* of God.

In confessing faith in the "one God," we are recognizing the *singularity* and *sufficiency* of God. In confessing faith in the "Father, the Almighty," we are recognizing the *supremacy* of God as the *source*. There are overlaps here between all these words, like notes in a chord that both harmonize and accentuate built-in resonances. In fact, God as "the Almighty" was sometimes depicted in art as a breastfeeding mother to show the sufficiency of God—an image that some scholars connect with the name we mentioned earlier, El Shaddai.

JUICEBOX THEOLOGY

It's easy to confess God as the source but much harder to live like we believe it. I remember a conversation with my youth pastor when I was a teen about a girl I liked. How did I know whether I liked her too much? I asked. He said I should think about whether she was the source of my affirmation and self-worth. Well, he unpacked it more than that. We talked about how much I was being affected by whether she liked me or not and if I needed her attention in order to feel better about myself. I'll never forget him reaching out his arm to my heart and making a vacuum cleaner–like sucking sound to illustrate that an unhealthy relationship is one where we go to a person primarily to get from them what we think we need. Simple but profound, isn't it?

Over the decades that have followed, I've realized how much the simple idea shows up in so many areas of life. A new job makes us happy, so we start acting as if the job is the source of our joy. A friendship or a relationship brings us comfort, so we fool ourselves into believing that friendship or relationship is the source of the comfort we feel. Even in my marriage of twenty-three years, I have to remind myself—often in the wake of frustrations that result from my impossible expectations of my wife—that she, amazing and steady as she is, is not the source of my peace.

Relationships, meaningful work, and the beauty of creation and of art are *conduits* of joy and peace and awe and comfort and more; they are not the *source*. All created things are what goodness comes *through*, but they are not where goodness comes *from*.

Imagine drinking from a juicebox with a straw. What if you were foolish enough to think that the juice came from the straw? You pull the straw from the juicebox and discard the carton. Initially, a few drops of juice are left in the straw, so you think you're a genius. Your hands are free, and you've still got juice since the straw is in your mouth. It would take only an instant before your joy turns to frustration. "This cursed straw," you might say. "You once brought me so much joy and happiness. But now, you just aren't filling me anymore!" But the straw was never where the juice came from; it was only what the juice came through.

This juicebox theology could wake us up from the lies we live. When a job isn't making us happy, when a spouse isn't bringing us joy, when a church has lost its luster, we discard them and chase after new straws. Maybe a new city, maybe a new job, maybe new friends, maybe then we'll find what we're looking for. But this, too, is much chasing after the wind (Eccl. 1:14). The teacher in Ecclesiastes knew. The good gifts of God are what goodness comes through, but they are not where goodness comes from.

Stay close to the source.

The best way I know to keep the straw in the juicebox, to remind ourselves of the source, is to practice gratitude. Psychologists say our brains remember negative experiences far more easily than positive ones. Some have called it "Teflon brain" (the good stuff just bounces right off) and "Velcro brain" (the bad stuff sticks).[2] It's got to be an effect of the fall, don't you think?

Because our brains are like this, we have to work harder and more intentionally at remembering the good. But more than that, for the Christian, gratitude doesn't just remind us of the gifts; gratitude returns us to the Giver.

THE MAKER OF . . . YOU

The final words of the first stanza of the Creed confess our belief in the "maker of heaven and earth, of all that is, seen and unseen." Once again there are overlapping shades of meaning here with the earlier phrases, underscoring God as the source and sovereign over all things—not just of the visible but of the invisible. To be clear, the invisible could refer to the spiritual realm, like angels and demons; but it could also refer to the abstract creational goods like the ones we named above: peace, joy, comfort, and more.

God is the Maker.

Note the language. He is not "the one who made." He is named as the Maker because that is who God is, not simply what God did. This line could easily be an echo of Colossians 1, which names Jesus as the one in whom "all things are held together" (Col. 1:17). The Creed names God as the *singular source*, the God of *sufficiency* and *supremacy*, and now the God who is also the *sustainer*.

These descriptions of God can all sound distant and abstract—some far away Being in the sky. It seems not too different from people who ask "the Universe" to send them good vibes. But the Bible talks about God the Maker in a very intimate way. The people of God in the Old Testament had a prayer that described the Creator in a deeply personal way:

> For you created my inmost being;
>> you knit me together in my mother's womb.
> I praise you because I am fearfully and
>> wonderfully made;
>> your works are wonderful,
>> I know that full well.
> My frame was not hidden from you
>> when I was made in the secret place,
>> when I was woven together in the depths of
>> the earth.
> Your eyes saw my unformed body;
>> all the days ordained for me were written in
>> your book
>> before one of them came to be.
> How precious to me are your thoughts, God!
>> How vast is the sum of them!

> Were I to count them,
>> they would outnumber the grains of sand—
>> when I awake, I am still with you. (Ps.
>> 139:13–18 NIV)

God, the Maker of heaven and earth, is the one who knit you together in the womb. He's the one who saw you and knew you, who sees you and knows you. He wove every part of who you are together. His thoughts are more numerous than the grains of sand.

Now stop right there. This prayer, this poem, was written by people who were surrounded by sand. Granted, it's not quite like beach sand, but still, sand has a way of sticking to you. I live minutes from the beach (try not to be jealous), and I aim to get to the beach at least once a week, if not more frequently. There's something about the water and the waves, the endless horizon, and yes, the sand around your toes. Imagine each grain as one of God's thoughts about you. Each one speaks of His affection, His love, His care, and His delight. And just as the sand sticks to you, so do God's thoughts about you.

Ancient creation myths, like the Enuma Elish, which Israelites would have heard from their neighboring countries or their neighbors when they were exiles in Babylon, tell a story of a male god who killed a female goddess and spread her guts to create the cosmos. Humans come from the blood of a lower god, and they exist only to be slaves to the gods. This was the dominant story when the Genesis narrative appeared in the world. We read Genesis and the story of creation and utilize it as ammunition against atheistic evolution. Christians are inundated with the arguments. Non-Christians are weary—and maybe *wary* as well—of all of it. But Genesis in its own day was startlingly good news. There is a God—one God, the only one. And He made everything—He made *you!*—on purpose and with pleasure.

In fact, in the Greek translation of the Old Testament, the Septuagint, which is the "Bible" Jesus and His disciples read, the word for *blessed* when God blessed the world He had made is *eulogeo*. If that sounds like *eulogy*, our word for a funeral reflection, that's because that's where the word comes from. *Eulogy* simply means "good words." We speak "good words" about people after they're gone, at the end of their lives. God spoke good words over you at the beginning of time.

I shared the following story in my 2019 book, *Blessed Broken Given*, but it is worth repeating here. When Holly and I had our first child, someone gave us the idea to begin to write in a journal for each child. At first, the entries were just observations: their favorite blankie, sleep quirks, favorite songs, and more. But as they became toddlers, we began writing what we *saw* in them: their gifts, their emerging personalities, the funny things they said and did. And then as they got older, the journal entries became letters. Most years, it was only one or two entries from Holly and me. But over time the entries added up to a fairly full journal.

On each child's thirteenth birthday, we took them out for breakfast and read portions of their journal to them and then let them have access to their journal so they could refer to it whenever they wanted. Holly and I continued to write in these journals until each child turned eighteen, at which point the journal was permanently passed into their possession. But the idea of letting them begin reading it at thirteen was so that the teen years would be full of voices that would try to shape them and influence them. We wanted our voices to be the loudest. We wanted them to know that we were there at the beginning, that we saw them and knew them.

To confess God as the Maker of all things is much bigger than being a parent. Yes, God is the Father. But as Creator of heaven and earth, of all that is, both seen and unseen, He is uniquely qualified to tell us the truth about ourselves. He was there. He knows. He sees. And He has a whole lot of good words to say about you.

PURPOSE AND PRESSURE

To confess God as the Maker is to answer humanity's search for meaning. If the best that the Enuma Elish could do was to paint humans as slaves of the gods with kings sitting precariously atop the hierarchy of mortals, then Genesis is a shocking claim. Humans were created on purpose *for a purpose.*

In her breathtakingly beautiful book *Being God's Image*, Carmen Imes points out that our "identity as God's image implies a representational role—the Creator God appointed humans to exercise his rule over creation on his behalf."[3] The Maker made us in His image. Being made in God's image means we have both *dignity* and *authority*.[4] Dignity is connected to our identity, our blessedness, and our belovedness, as we discussed earlier. But authority is about meaning; it's connected to our purpose.

The poet-prophet Isaiah, writing to remind Israel of their vocation, connected the Creator God with the Calling God: the God who made you, made you for a reason.

> God the LORD says—
>> the one who created the heavens,
>> the one who stretched them out,
>> the one who spread out the earth and its
>>> offspring,
>> the one who gave breath to its people
>> and life to those who walk on it—
> I, the LORD, have called you for a good reason.
>> I will grasp your hand and guard you,
>> and give you as a covenant to the people,
>> as a light to the nations,
>> to open blind eyes, to lead the prisoners from
>>> prison,
>> and those who sit in darkness from the
>>> dungeon. (Isa. 42:5–7)

Let's make this as plain as possible: Meaning is received, not made. We are not the Maker. All human attempts to make meaning of our lives apart from the Maker fall short. More than that, the very attempt at meaning-making without the Maker places too great a burden on our shoulders. For a few generations now, Americans have sought to live out the creed that every person ought to be free to create not only their own future but also their own meaning, their own truth, and even their own reality. In the past few decades, the rise of individualism is noticeable even through the popularity of key phrases. Noted sociologist and scholar of generational patterns Jean Twenge wrote, "Assuming verbal language mirrored written language, Boomers growing up in the 1950s were only rarely told 'just be yourself' or 'you're special,' but Millennials and Gen Z'ers heard these phrases much more often."[5]

Yet, later in her monumental project, Twenge noted about Gen Z that "every indicator of mental health and psychological well-being has become more negative among teens and young adults since 2012."[6] For Twenge, there are several contributing factors, but chief among them in her estimation is the rise of technology. "The very large and sudden changes in mental health and behavior between Millennials and Gen Z are likely not a coincidence," she argued. "They arose from the fastest adoption of any technology in human history."[7]

Put these two factors together: hyper-individualism and technology. Technology has the power to connect. But it also has the power to turn the mirror—or more accurately, the camera—on ourselves. We become the center of the story. The way reality TV shows disrupted network television in the early 2000s by making ordinary people the stars of the show is nothing compared to the way YouTube, Instagram, and TikTok disrupted all media by making each of us the star of our own show.

All of this leaves me to wonder about the weight of this alleged freedom. Does the pursuit of defining our own reality and making our own meaning hold out the promise of liberation but turn out to be the worst kind of oppression? Like Thor's hammer, which none are worthy to carry (except for Captain America eventually), is the pen for writing our own story too great a weight for us to bear? What happens when we write ourselves into a corner? What happens when we make mistakes, as we surely will? Who can erase the ink or redeem the narrative?

Faith in God as the Maker is not blind acquiescence to a distant deity. It is loving surrender to a loving God, a God who sees us and knows us, a God who made us on purpose for a purpose. To confess faith in a Maker is to turn over the pen, to surrender our story, and to receive our *identity, dignity,* and *authority* from God Himself.

Tie It Together

We believe in one God,
the Father, the Almighty
the maker of heaven and earth,
of all that is, seen and unseen.

What does it mean to believe these words?

- It means that we believe God is the singular, sufficient, sovereign, and supreme source of all there is. He is the only one; He is enough; He is over all; He is the best; and He is the originator.

- It means that God alone is God. I am not. You are not. They are not. It is not.

What does it mean to live by these words?

- It means that we refuse to treat things that are not God as if they were.

- It means that we resist the temptation to shape God into our image. Instead, we live like God is enough.

  - We turn to God as the source.

  - We hear His words of blessing and love.

  - We walk in His purpose for our lives.

CHAPTER 5

The World's True Lord

We believe in one Lord, Jesus Christ,
the only Son of God,
eternally begotten of the Father,
God from God, Light from Light,
true God from true God,
begotten, not made,
of one Being with the Father.
Through him all things were made.

ChatGPT won't tell you who the most influential person in human history is without giving you a list of requisite caveats. "Determining the most important figures in human history is subjective and varies based on different perspectives." Blah, blah, blah. *It's a simple question,* I thought. But it took some work to figure out the right questions to ask. For example, when I asked who the most *important* person in history is, Jesus didn't crack the top ten. That list is reserved for Alexander the Great, Leonardo da Vinci, Isaac Newton, Albert Einstein, Mahatma Gandhi, Nelson Mandela, Marie Curie, William Shakespeare, Martin Luther King Jr., and Winston Churchill.

But after a bit of conversation with OpenAI about where Jesus would rank and whether Jesus would actually be the most *famous* person in history, it started to give me the answer it thought I was looking for. From that point on, no matter how I phrased the question—Who is the most influential . . . ? Who is the most significant . . . ? Who is the most important . . . ?—the list came back with Jesus in pole position each time.

That's how questions of significance and importance and influence work, isn't it? It's subjective. The answer depends on who's asking. The individual decides who matters *to them* and who doesn't.

Unless, of course, there were some claim to a fixed reality, to an inherent and intrinsic quality that marked a person as unequivocally the single most significant, important, and influential person who ever lived. But that hardly seems possible. Such categories are reserved for . . . well, *God.* But God isn't a human. God isn't technically *in* human history. *Right?*

When you approach the question this way, you may begin

to see just what marks out the uniqueness of Christ. Jesus is, Christians believe, God who came in human flesh. Jesus is God who came to do for us what we so desperately needed and deeply longed for but could not do for ourselves. Fully human, yet fully God. Incarnate, yet eternal.

Is He the most important person in human history? Well, yes, but. Yes, but He's not *merely* human and He wasn't always *in* human history. He was before history and beyond it and will one day bring history to its close and culmination.

So maybe my question wasn't so simple after all. You can hardly blame ChatGPT for getting it wrong at first.

THE ONLY SAVING KING

In the Nicene Creed, the stanza about Jesus divides pretty naturally into three sections. The first section focuses on His divinity, while the second and the third are about His humanity. Or more precisely, the second section of the Jesus stanza is about the incarnation, while the third section is about His crucifixion, resurrection, ascension, and return.

Taken together, it's far and away the longest stanza of the three that make up the Creed and for good reason. The central topic of conversation was the nature of Jesus Christ, arguably the controversy that necessitated the convening of the bishops for the Council of Nicaea. That does not mean there was chaotic disagreement. In fact, the council agreed on who Jesus was with a notable exception: Arius and a few of his followers.

But the council settled what the other church leaders already believed. And *they* believed what had been passed down to them from the apostles and leaders of the early church, not only through personal witness but through their writings, which were eventually collected as the New Testament. So if the words and phrases of this stanza about Jesus sound familiar, it may be because you've encountered them in the Bible. Many are directly lifted from John 1, Colossians 1, Hebrews 1, and more.

The opening titles for Jesus seem superfluous. You might even read over them quickly to get to the verbs, where the action is. But each title is significant. More than that, each title actually underscores the same key element of Jesus' nature. It's a triple underscore, a triad of emphasis, making one dramatic claim.

Lord

We know that *Lord* is shorthand for "Israel's God." The Israelites would not pronounce the four letters—transliterated in English as YHWH—that stood for God's covenantal name. Instead, they would say *Adonai*, which means "lord." Many Bible translations signal this by translating *YHWH* as LORD in small caps to indicate the holiness of God's name.

But *Lord* had another reference point in the early Christian centuries, a reference that would have been well known far beyond Jewish circles. Lord was what the emperor called himself—or rather, what he wanted everyone to call him. Caesar was the "kyrios," the Lord.

By the time the council met to pen the words of the Creed, the emperor was a Christian. Indeed, the council was convened at his instigation. So perhaps the naming of Jesus as Lord did not have the same political bravado as it would have had in earlier centuries. Imagine Paul before the destruction of Jerusalem and under the nose of the fearsome and erratic emperor Nero saying that Jesus is Lord! Nevertheless, part of the potency of naming Jesus as Lord in the first line of the stanza about Him is precisely because it carried imperial overtones: Jesus is the King! More than that, by confessing, "We believe in *one* Lord," His followers were saying that He is the one and only King. No other lord, no other king, no other kingdom or empire.

Christ

One of my all-time favorite N. T. Wright quips is that "Christ" is not Jesus' surname, as if His parents were "Joseph Christ" and "Mary Christ," and there was little baby Jesus Christ. It never fails to get a laugh, even when I say it. It's stating the obvious. But what is perhaps less obvious is what *Christ* actually refers to. *Christ* or *Christos* is the Greek version of the Hebrew title *messiah*. Both mean "anointed one." Isaiah, more than any other Old Testament source, fills out our vision of what the Messiah would do. But it was Hannah who sang about it first.

The fulfillment, the way 1 Samuel tells it, is David. David was the anointed king, the one who finally defeated Israel's long-standing enemy, the Philistines, who loomed large over them with threats and attacks of violence and death. Furthermore, David was a *representational* king—he stood in for the nation as a young man and defeated the Philistine giant-warrior Goliath. This is why the title "Son of David," which is used in a few places in the Gospels, is another way of saying "the Messiah." The Messiah is the chosen king who would win a great and decisive victory on behalf of God's people.

So far, the titles show Jesus to be the *exclusive* and *ultimate emperor-king* and the *representative* and *victorious king*. But there's one more royal reference in the Creed's titles for Jesus.

Son of God

Most Christians assume that "Son of God" is a reference to the divinity of Jesus. True enough. But a closer look at how the Bible uses this title reveals another layer. Adam is called the "Son of God" in Luke's genealogy. And why not? Adam and Eve, as we said before, were made in God's image. They carried, as all humans are meant to, both *kinship* and *kingship*, in Carmen Imes's marvelous summary.[1]

Who else is called the "Son of God"? Israel is referred to in Exodus as God's firstborn, hence the parallels of striking Egypt's firstborn sons as a sign to release the Israelites from slavery. And then—the plot thickens—Israel's king is called the Son of God in the Psalms (Ps. 2:7–8 and Ps. 110).

So "Son of God" is a biblical way of saying the human representative of God on earth, made to reflect His rule and reign. There it is again: a kingly reference.

Jesus

Amid these titles is the name given to the incarnate Son of God per the angelic instruction: *Jesus*. Or in Hebrew, *Yeshua*, meaning "the Lord saves."

Put the titles all together and we begin to see there is only one who is the *exclusive, representative* King—who represents the people before their enemies and God before His people—who wins a great *victory* and establishes God's *rule* on earth. *Who could possibly do that?* It's little wonder that no king of Israel ever lived up to the job. But they sketch the outline of an office that God Himself planned from the beginning to fill.

Who is this King of glory? The Lord strong and mighty, YHWH Himself who has come to save. That's who Jesus is.

We can say all this even more succinctly. What does it mean to confess Jesus as the Lord, the Christ, and the Son of God? It means we are announcing that *Jesus is the saving King*.

ALLEGIANCE ALONE

How do we respond to this saving King? If the key for Christianity becoming credible is for Christians to live as if their Creed is true, then it is not enough to confess Jesus as the saving King; we have to live like He is. What does that look like?

Let's start with perhaps a more basic question: How do you respond to a king?

On Saturday, May 6, 2023, the United Kingdom crowned

His Majesty King Charles III alongside Camilla as the queen consort. It had been seventy years since the coronation of a British monarch. While the British Empire no longer exists, the ceremony for King Charles III was viewed by almost as many people as there were in the empire at its peak, thanks in no small part to technology. An estimated four hundred million people worldwide watched as a king took the throne.

But the controversy leading up to the ceremony centered on a few key words: a pledge of allegiance. The tradition had been for royal princes and peers to kneel as a form of homage and take an oath of allegiance to the monarch. But the archbishop of Canterbury had reimagined this moment. Instead of an "homage of peers," there would be an "homage of the people," where "all persons of goodwill in the United Kingdom of Great Britain and Northern Ireland, and of the other realms and the territories to make their homage, in heart and voice, to their undoubted King, defender of all."[2] And the specific words they would be invited to say were "I swear that I will pay true allegiance to Your Majesty, and to your heirs and successors, according to law. So help me God."

The innovation created a stir, not just because the Brits are precious about their traditions, but because such words seemed to fly in the face of modern democratic sensibilities. As one outspoken critic of the monarchy put it, "In a democracy it is the head of state who should be swearing allegiance to the people, not the other way around. This kind of nonsense should have died with Elizabeth I, not outlived Elizabeth II."[3]

The archbishop pushed back by saying, "In every Anglican

service, every Christian service, it is normal for congregations to participate. It's an invitation, so if you want to join in at this point, by all means do so. If you don't want to, that's fine. There's no drama to it."[4] In the end, the people were given the option of simply saying, "God save King Charles." The homage of allegiance was to be an invitation, not an expectation or a command.

The whole controversy is a window into how modern societies in the twenty-first century don't easily embrace kings. Kings in our world cannot command allegiance. They can only invite it. And if you'd rather not give allegiance, you can simply pray for the king.

Humorous as it may be, this reluctance to give allegiance to a king is in fact how many Christians approach Jesus. Jesus is King. Sure, it's a nice title. And we're fine to give Him all the pomp and circumstance of Christmas and Easter. After all, those occasions have sentimental value. But like the people of Britain, we'd rather the King pledge allegiance to us than commit our fidelity to Him. So we're good on the gospel so long as by *gospel* we mean Jesus died for our sins. We believe that. And if faith is about believing, then it's all fine since we're happy to believe such good news.

But if the gospel announcement is more startling, more arresting, more scandalous, and if we really are saying that Jesus (and not Caesar or you or me or anyone else) is the saving King, then mere belief is hardly a fitting response. The only way to respond to such an announcement is with *allegiance*.

This is exactly what Matthew Bates (along with a host

of other scholars from Scot McKnight to N. T. Wright and others) argue for when they call us to understand faith as "allegiance" and not mere mental assent. The word for *faith* in the New Testament is *pistis*, and Bates argues that it can mean allegiance, though it doesn't have to, nor does it always, nor is it its central conceptual meaning. But—and here's the key—when the word is used within the framework of royalty or kingship, it means allegiance or fidelity. In his summary at the end of his book *Gospel Allegiance*, Bates wrote this under the heading "Our Response to the Gospel":

> Allegiance alone. Allegiance is expressed in repentance, trusting loyalty, and baptism. Repentance from sins means revoking other allegiances so as to live in the way Jesus commands. Saving faith is loyalty to Jesus as the forgiving king and includes good deeds done through the power of the Holy Spirit.[5]

Allegiance alone. For some of you, this is the moment to turn from your career or your bank account or your relationships as saving king. We'd never say that those things are our king, of course. But how we live may tell another story. What gets to orient our time and attention? What orders our priorities? What is the lens through which we make decisions? Allegiance is much more than honor or homage. It is surrender and service. By that measure, maybe the greatest rival to Jesus' kingship is *ourselves*. We are most prone to put ourselves on the throne. It's our default mode.

But confessing belief in Jesus as the "one Lord . . . Christ . . . Son of God" is to proclaim Him as the only saving King. Such a confession is not a neutral statement. It's not an observation as if we were saying, "The weather is nice today." It's much more like saying, "Your company got bought out!" or "Your house is on fire!" or "Your flight is leaving now!" It's an announcement that alters reality; it's a confession that changes the conditions you've been living under. *Breaking news! Everything is different now.* It's news that demands a response. And with news about a king, the only fitting response is allegiance.

To say the Creed is to surrender our lordship. It is to set aside our agenda. It means we stop hedging our bets. It's Jesus alone who deserves the throne. And our faith is the pledge of our whole lives bowing down and bending low in allegiance.

THE ETERNAL SON

After naming Jesus with particular and significant titles, the Creed goes on to describe more about the very nature of the Son of God:

> . . . eternally begotten of the Father,
> God from God, Light from Light,
> true God from true God,
> begotten, not made,
> of one Being with the Father.
> Through him all things were made.

Embedded in these poetic lines is rich early Christology. But the leaders at the Council of Nicaea were not pulling these words out of the air. They were drawing deeply from the early Christian documents we call the New Testament.

When they wrote that Jesus was "of one Being with the Father" and used the imagery of light, they were echoing what John wrote: "And the Word was with God and the Word was God. The Word was with God in the beginning. . . . The true light that shines on all people was coming into the world" (John 1:1–2, 9).

And when they wrote about Jesus being the one through whom all things were made, they were giving voice to what John, Paul, and the writer of Hebrews said about Him:

Everything came into being through the Word, and without the Word nothing came into being. (John 1:3)

The Son is the image of the invisible God, the one who is first over all creation, because all things were created by him: both in the heavens and on the earth, the things that are visible and the things that are invisible. Whether they are thrones or powers, or rulers or authorities, all things were created through him and for him. He existed before all things, and all things are held together in him. (Col. 1:15–17)

In the past God spoke to our ancestors through the prophets at many times and in various ways, but in these last

days he has spoken to us by his Son, whom he appointed
heir of all things, and through whom also he made the
universe. The Son is the radiance of God's glory and the
exact representation of his being, sustaining all things by
his powerful word. (Heb. 1:1–3 NIV)

These claims about Jesus were even more stunning than
the first claim about His kingship. Now they were clearly and
unequivocally confessing His divinity. They were naming the
oneness of the Son with the Father and specifying a few qualities of God shared by the Son: uncreated, eternal, light, creator,
and sustainer.

In the next few lines, we will come to confess Jesus as the
incarnate Son of God, but here we bow before Jesus as the *eternal Son of God*.

This can be hard to imagine—precisely because of the
incarnation. Our image of Jesus is shaped by art and films
and TV shows that show the incarnate Son of God. But Jesus
is not only fully human; He is also fully God.

Consider how John in his revelation described his vision
of Jesus:

I turned to see who was speaking to me, and when I turned,
I saw . . . someone who looked like the Human One. He
wore a robe that stretched down to his feet, and he had a
gold sash around his chest. His head and hair were white
as white wool—like snow—and his eyes were like a fiery
flame. His feet were like fine brass that has been purified

in a furnace, and his voice sounded like rushing water. He held seven stars in his right hand, and from his mouth came a sharp, two-edged sword. His appearance was like the sun shining with all its power. (Rev. 1:12, 13–16)

That is not a character to be casual about. John recorded his own response: "When I saw him, I fell at his feet like a dead man" (Rev. 1:17). I'm old enough to remember the first round of attempts at making Jesus relatable. Phrases like "Jesus is my homeboy" or "Jesus is my BFF" are well-intentioned and perhaps even helpful to someone who feels distant from God. But while we may begin our awareness of Jesus by recognizing His nearness, we must not stay there. We are not praying to "dashboard Jesus." We are worshiping the uncreated Creator and Sustainer of all things—the eternal Son. If we really catch that vision of Jesus, then like John, we will fall to our knees!

HE HOLDS IT ALL

But terror is not the main response to the eternal Son of God. In fact, fear is not even the intended response. When John fell like a dead man, Jesus put His right hand on John. Why His *right hand*? Your guess might be that the right hand denotes authority and power, and you would not be wrong. But the picture is more particular than a generic notion of authority and power. In the verse right before it, John described Jesus as holding the seven stars in His right hand.

Think of it: The one who holds the stars and the galaxies holds your life! To use the phrases of Paul and the author of Hebrews, the one who "holds all things together" and "sustains all things" is holding and sustaining you!

That is why Jesus said to John, "Don't be afraid. I'm the first and the last, and the living one. I was dead, but look! Now I'm alive forever and always. I have the keys of Death and the Grave" (Rev. 1:17–18). These are words of comfort, words of assurance, words of victory and authority. Jesus is the beginning and the end. Jesus is the risen one, the one who has conquered death. When He says, "Don't be afraid," He means it. After all, nothing starts without Him. Nothing ends without Him. Not even death and the grave can stop Him. What else is there? Life and death and everything in between—Jesus is over it all.

This makes me want to worship, not simply in reverent awe but in grateful adoration. As it turns out, after hearing Jesus' message to the churches, worship is exactly the next thing John experienced.

Where are you right now? *Where* are you? In life, in your soul, in this moment? Are you afraid? Are you tired? Are you feeling shaky and unsure? That is what life does to us. Everything on earth is fragile and fraught. But Jesus is not simply the Human One. He is the eternal Son. He is before time and beyond time, before this world and beyond this world. All time and matter and space and nature—all that is— came to being through Him and is sustained by Him.

Do not be afraid. Even when life is falling apart, even when *you* are falling apart, Jesus knows how to hold it all together. Jesus knows how to hold *you* together. You don't have to be eternal. You don't have to be transcendent. You don't have to be godlike. That was the first temptation in the garden, the lie that said we have to be more than we are; the myth that we can shed our limits and transcend our nature. No, you don't have to be divine. You can be perfectly human-sized, a phrase my friend and author-speaker Steve Cuss is fond of using. There is only one human who is eternal, only one who was before all that is and who will be forever. His name is Jesus.

The more we embrace our humanness, the more the transcendence of Jesus becomes good news. These are not lines of doctrine; they are lyrics for worship.

Tie It Together

We believe in one Lord, Jesus Christ,
the only Son of God,
eternally begotten of the Father,
God from God, Light from Light,
true God from true God,
begotten, not made,
of one Being with the Father.
Through him all things were made.

What does it mean to believe these words?

- It means announcing Jesus as the saving King.

- It means acknowledging Jesus as the eternal Son of God.

- It means recognizing that Jesus is God who came to save us and reign over all.

What does it mean to live by these words?

- It means we pledge our allegiance to Jesus and Jesus alone. We dethrone all other kings, beginning with ourselves. We allow our will to be displaced, ourselves to be moved off-center so that Jesus can take His rightful place (which is another way of saying *we worship*).

- These words are a call to worship Jesus, to fall before Him in reverence and surrender.

- Jesus is the saving King and the eternal Son. Fall before Him in faithful *allegiance*, reverent *awe*, and grateful *adoration*.

CHAPTER 6

The Story Above All Stories

For us men and for our salvation
he came down from heaven:
by the power of the Holy Spirit
he became incarnate from the Virgin
Mary, and was made man.
For our sake he was crucified
under Pontius Pilate;
he suffered death and was buried.

I am sitting in the café of a big box bookstore like it's 1999. Back then, these behemoth booksellers were cast as the villain, as in my favorite rom-com of all time, *You've Got Mail*. But these days, any brick-and-mortar place where I can be surrounded by books and sit leisurely with them is a treasure.

What's a Christian, Anyway?

Something about it makes me smile. I've just browsed several rows of books—some of them religious, most not. Some are nonfiction; others are fiction. And then there are memoirs that surely live somewhere in between. All of them are trying to stand out to the casual browser. And all are, in some form, a story. The story of an idea, the story of a life, the story of a city or a company and more.

Humans are storytelling creatures. It is how we make sense of the world; it's how we make meaning of our lives. And there is something of a template for the stories we tell. There is a line, variously attributed but perhaps most often to the great Russian novelist Leo Tolstoy, though I have not seen it cited, that "all great literature is one of two stories: A man goes on a journey or a stranger comes to town."

Many have remarked that if this were true, then it could also be argued there is really only one story told from two perspectives—for the man who goes on a journey is also a stranger who comes to someone else's town. Even if we didn't reduce it that way, think of some great stories that connect these themes:

- Bilbo Baggins goes on a journey *because* Gandalf, a stranger, comes to town.
- Harry Potter goes to Hogwarts and begins his quest to defeat Voldemort because an owl (or rather, many owls!) comes to town (and eventually because Hagrid comes to the remote lighthouse cabin where the Dursleys seek to escape).

- *Little Women*, a favorite with my wife and daughters (and let's be honest, a favorite of mine too), is arguably about Jo's journey to find herself after deciding against marriage to Teddy, who initially was the stranger who came to town.

Anyway, I'm not convinced that *all* stories can be meaningfully reduced to these two themes. But there is something fascinating about searching for the repeated themes human stories seem to trace.

For Christians, there is one story that stands behind all stories: the story of God coming to us in human flesh, to be for us what we are not, to do for us what we cannot; the God who suffered with us, as us, for us; the God who died; the God who was raised up in victory, having gone through death to resurrection life. This is a story that pulls together all human stories. It makes sense of our longing; it accounts for our failure and our frailty; it offers us a hope beyond ourselves, a redemption outside our reach; it answers the dream of life that goes beyond death.

But maybe the ubiquity of the Jesus story is the very reason some reject it. After all, is this not some version of an old human myth or of several myths? C. S. Lewis, acquainted with myth because of his academic field of medieval literature, referred to Christianity as "a myth which is also a fact."[1] What he meant is there was an old myth of a "dying God" that happened "at a particular date, in a particular place, followed by definable historical consequences."[2] These parallels ought not make one nervous, Lewis argued. In fact, "they ought to be there—it would be a stumbling block if they weren't."

It could be that Lewis had in mind what the writer of Ecclesiastes referred to as God putting "eternity in [our] hearts" (Eccl. 3:11). These myths exist for a reason; they are clues from our own longing. Yet the key in Christianity is that God *actually came* into our world. Lewis put it this way: "For this is the marriage of heaven and earth: perfect myth and perfect fact: claiming not only our love and our obedience, but also our wonder and delight, addressed to the savage, the child, and the poet in each one of us no less than to the moralist, the scholar, and the philosopher."

Christian confession of Jesus is not only the marriage of heaven and earth in the sense of what Lewis called myth and fact. It is also because the confession of who Jesus is links the *eternal Son* with the *incarnate Son*. The one who was before all things and through whom all things were made is the one and the same who came into the world that He made. John put it this way in the opening lines of his Gospel account: "In the beginning was the Word and the Word was with God and the Word was God. The Word was with God in the beginning. Everything came into being through the Word, and without the Word nothing came into being. . . . The Word became flesh and made his home among us" (John 1:1–3, 14).

Jesus creating all things and then coming into creation to redeem; Jesus coming to earth for us, dying for our sin, rising in victory—this is the heart of the Creed and the center of our faith. It is the story of all stories, and because it is the myth that is also true, it captures our wonder and our worship.

FOR US

The entire confession of faith turns on the first two words of this section: *"For us . . ."*

For us. For you. For me. Everything that comes next is personal. It's not abstract; it's not an idea or a concept. It is *for us*. This is the first time we are referenced; we are the object of a phrase. Something is about us; something is for us! This is where we enter the story.

I have a close friend who told me how his father-in-law would frequently talk to him about the ins and outs of his business. My friend would politely listen and try to ask a few occasional questions to seem moderately interested. But mostly he was just trying to pass the time and make small talk. He knew his father-in-law loved his work and was passionate about the company, but it was such a different field from his own work that he didn't ever pay too close attention. Then one day, his father-in-law told him he was retiring, and more than that, one day the business would be passed on to his wife, and by extension to him. He was shocked, not at the news but at his own daftness. He should've seen it coming. He realized that all the talk, all the insight and insider information, was for a reason. The business was *for him*!

Something similar is going on with the Creed. Up until

this point, a person may zone out. The Father, the Almighty . . . *yes, yes,* you might think. All good information to know. But then all of a sudden the words appear: "For us . . ." We wake from our stupor. We start paying attention. And just in time. For everything that follows is for our sake. The incarnation, the crucifixion, the death, and the burial—it was all for us, for our salvation, for our sake.

It's hard for that truth to really sink in. When I was a boy, my mother tried talking to me about how Jesus died for me. Analytical child that I was, I replied that Jesus had died for the whole world. "Yes," she said patiently, "but it was for you specifically. Jesus died *for you.*" "But John 3:16," I argued, "says, 'For God so loved the world.' It wasn't just for me. God loves everyone." My mother knew, of course, that I was *technically* correct but was in danger of missing the personal power of the gospel. "Yes, God loves the whole world. But He loves *you.* And He died *for you.*"

I still get emotional thinking about that. As a preacher, it's far easier to tell everyone else how God loves *them,* how Jesus died *for them.* But the truth is, he died *for me.*

Think of Paul, the great theologian and pastor, the brilliant preacher of the power of the gospel. In the midst of his theologically dense and polemical letter to the Galatians, Paul zoomed in from his sweeping panoramic vision of the restoration of creation, the renewal of covenant, and the redemption of Jews and Gentiles together to say, "I have been crucified with Christ and I no longer live, but Christ lives in me. And the life that I now live in my body, I live by faith, indeed, by the faithfulness of God's Son, *who loved me and gave himself for me*" (Gal. 2:20, emphasis added). Jesus who loved *me*. Down from the lofty heights of doctrine, freezing the frame of the camera in the vast drama of God's salvation, we see ourselves standing before Jesus—fully and truly loved.

But who is the "us"? There's a voice in our heads that quickly disqualifies us. "Sure, that might be *you*, but it's probably not *me*."

I find it significant that the early Christians who wrote the words of the Creed mention two names in this stanza on Jesus. These two human names are the only human names in the entire confession of faith. The Creed is unapologetically about Father, Son, and Holy Spirit—why would there be human names? Yet, the very paragraph that describes the incarnation of the second person of the Trinity mentions the names of two humans. See the words again with the names italicized for emphasis:

> For us men and for our salvation
> he came down from heaven:
> by the power of the Holy Spirit
> he became incarnate from the *Virgin Mary*, and
> was made man.
> For our sake he was crucified under *Pontius Pilate*;
> he suffered death and was buried.

Mary and Pilate. The peasant girl and the politician. The powerless and the powerful. The oppressed and the oppressor. The lowly and the mighty. The humble and the proud. Certainly, they play different roles in the story, yet both are named here. Mary is venerated ever so slightly with the adjective *Virgin*, emphasizing the miraculous nature of her pregnancy. But Pilate is not vilified. I wonder if it's because the early Christians, watching even Constantine slowly turning toward faith, held out hope that anyone could be saved, no matter their associations or past or wickedness or status.

From the low to the highest of the high, and for everyone in between, Jesus came. This is the "us" in the "for us."

Even those who think they are rich are really poor; and those who think they are well are actually in need of a physician; and those who think they see are, in reality, blind. This is a theme repeated in the Gospels. There is no virtue that earns the gift of Jesus Christ, and there is no wickedness that disqualifies us from receiving Him. It was for us—all of us—that He came.

AND FOR OUR SALVATION

The question we must ask when we contemplate the coming of Jesus for us is *Why?* Why did He come? What was the goal of the incarnation?

He did this for us *and* for our *salvation*. In the sentence about the cross, the early Christians said it one more time: "For our sake he was crucified." Christ came for us and for our salvation; Christ was crucified for our sake.

Now we must begin to connect these two things: us and our salvation. Christ's coming *and* Christ's death were for us *and* for our salvation. This salvation for which Christ came was attained through the death, burial, and resurrection of Jesus Christ. We will say more about the resurrection, the ascension, and return in the next chapter. Here we will look briefly at the cross. For all the atonement theories and human attempts—and there are many fruitful metaphors and paradigms—at understanding the meaning of the cross, we cannot move beyond the core of early Christian confession. A couple of centuries before the Council of Nicaea, Paul wrote to the Corinthians about a kind of early "rule of faith," a sort of proto-confession.

> I passed on to you as most important what I also received: Christ died for our sins in line with the scriptures, he was buried, and he rose on the third day in line with the scriptures. (1 Cor. 15:3–4)

Why do we need salvation? What did we need saving from? The way this verse puts it, Jesus died for our *sins*—for all our failures and fractures, for all the ways we have sinned against God and against each other.

But *sin* is a strange word. What does it mean? In the Bible sin is both a *failure* and a *power*. It is at its heart a failure of vocation, as N. T. Wright has argued.[3] Our vocation, our calling, was to live as image-bearers in God's world, to be the priests and viceroys in the world. Like an angled mirror, our calling as humans is to reflect creation's praise upward to God and God's wise and loving rule downward and outward into the world. But when humans decided not to be content with being God's image but to attempt to be God, it was like the moon insisting on becoming the sun. It was a sin of pride, of rebellion, of living apart from and against God. And at its core it was a failure, a failure of vocation. This is how Paul put it in Romans: "All have sinned and fall short of God's glory" (Rom. 3:23).

This failure is not individual or private. It is a failure that leads to a fracture. Sociologists describe human relationships as a kind of interactive chain that gets reinforced in communal rituals.[4] But when one person fails to do their part, the chain is broken. There is a kind of healthy shame, or shame that is proportionately related to guilt, that results from the breach of solidarity.

To put it in theological language, sin is never *only* personal or between you and God. Sin is always social as well. You see this in the Genesis story. Adam and Eve sinned against God, but the fracture between the divine-human relationship quickly splintered into more breaks. They hid from God—together. But as soon as God arrived, they turned on each other, the man blaming the woman and the woman blaming the serpent. In the very next chapter, we read of the fracture between brothers with Cain brutally murdering Abel.

A short while later, we read of the ground breaking with the waters of the deep and the heavens breaking open with torrential rains. The human relationship with the natural world was itself breaking, just as God had said it would with the metaphor of thorns and thistles. And then, finally, in Genesis 11, we read of societies splintering at Babel. If Babel was an attempt by humans to organize themselves apart from God and against God, even that attempt implicitly involved exploitation and slaves in the building of the tower.

Sins against God become sins against each other, if not in the same moment, then in its subsequent effects. This is why when Jesus was asked what the greatest commandment is, He did not split the vertical from the horizontal. He answered, *"You must love the Lord your God with all your heart, with all your being, with all your strength, and with all your mind, and love your neighbor as yourself"* (Luke 10:27). Sin is a failure to live up to this calling.

But sin is much more than just a failure. That can make it sound passive. The Bible uses many different words for sin—some that show much more active participation in sin, from transgressing boundaries to indulging in wickedness to embracing outright evil. The Anglican Prayer of Confession in the *Book of Common Prayer* tries to get the vertical and the horizontal *and* the active and passive forms of sin by leading us to pray:

Most merciful God, we confess that we have sinned against you in thought, word, and deed, by what we have done, and by what we have left undone. We have not loved you with our whole heart; we have not loved our neighbors as our-selves. We are truly sorry and we humbly repent.

So, to be clear, I am using *failure* in a very broad sense to cover all that ground of what we have done and what we have left undone. That admittedly may be an oversimplification. Still, even beyond that, sin is more than the wrong that we do. Sin, as the Bible describes it, is not just a failure; it is also a *power* we were under. Listen to how Paul went on to talk about sin:

- Sin entered the world through a human's sin (Rom. 5:12).
- Sin ruled in death (Rom. 5:21).
- We became slaves to sin (Rom. 6:6, 16–17) and under its power (Rom. 6:7, 14).
- Sin seized an opportunity through the Law to introduce death (Rom. 7:11).

But Paul was clear that because of Jesus—the salvation that He brings—we no longer *have* to be slaves to sin. How was sin's power broken? A few lines after announcing that there is *now* no condemnation for those who are in Christ Jesus, Paul told us that sin, the power we were under, was "condemned . . . in the body" of Christ Jesus. God did this "by sending his own Son to deal with sin in the same body as humans, who are controlled by sin" (Rom. 8:3).

To sum it all up: The death of Jesus on the cross achieved our salvation by dealing with sin (our failure) and Sin (the power we were under). That is not a temporary deliverance or a fictional salvation. It is a total and full healing of the fractures and the breaks in our lives and in our world caused by sin/Sin. If sin is the breaking apart of God's good world, then salvation is God putting it all back together again—beginning with us.

INTO THE PIT AND OUT

The death of Jesus on the cross is not all that the early Christians include in this paragraph. They say that he "suffered death" and "was buried." There's one more question we must address: Why the repetition of saying, "he was crucified . . . suffered death and was buried"? Is it poetry the early Christians were after? That would not be a bad reason.

I think these phrases were used together as a way of saying, "Jesus went all the way to the bottom." He fully and truly died. He didn't fake it or pretend to suffer. He actually suffered and died and was buried. He experienced *all* of human life, even its painful, lonely, and bitter end. There is nothing in the human experience that Jesus, the incarnate Son of God, did not also experience, which means there is nothing in the human experience that cannot be redeemed. It can all be saved.

There's a great scene in one of my all-time favorite TV shows, *The West Wing*. Leo, the chief of staff, is talking with Josh Lyman about his recent therapy session, a new experience for Josh and one he was more or less forced to endure because of a drinking problem that had surfaced to a small group of his friends. Josh is ashamed, frustrated, and tormented by the feeling of despair. There are childhood traumas he needs to face, pain that he can't erase, and he's not sure he can get through it. Right now, he just feels stuck.

And so Leo, picking up all of this from a brief exchange with Josh, begins to tell him a story.

> This guy's walking down the street when he falls in a hole. The walls are so steep, he can't get out. A doctor passes by, and the guy shouts up, "Hey you, can you help me out?" The doctor writes a prescription, throws it down in the hole, and moves on. Then a priest comes along, and the guy shouts up, "Father, I'm down in this hole; can you help me out?" The priest writes out a prayer, throws it down in the hole, and moves on. Then a friend walks by. "Hey Joe, it's me, can you help me out?" And the friend jumps in the hole. Our guy says, "Are you nuts? Now we're both down here." The friend says, "Yeah, but I've been down here before, and I know the way out."[5]

Jesus went into the pit, literally and figuratively, so that He could be with us and so that He could show us the way out. It was for us and for our salvation.

THROUGH US TO THE WORLD

In the classic Dickens novel *Great Expectations*, the orphan Pip comes to be the recipient of a great fortune. With the fortune comes the ability to become a proper gentlemen. His motive for his reinvention of self is to win the heart of Estella, a young woman who lives with the enigmatic Miss Havisham and with whom he has fallen in love. Yet Estella is merely acting on the instructions of Miss Havisham, who is toying with Pip as a sort of revenge against all men for her own experience of a broken heart.

But the turning point of the novel is when Pip discovers the source of his fortune. Until this moment, he had assumed it had been Miss Havisham granting him a certain modicum of wealth so that he might become worthy of Estella. As it turns out, the money was being sent from a former convict who had made something of his life in Australia, a convict to whom Pip had shown great kindness at the beginning of the story.

The question I think Dickens wanted his readers to wrestle with is whether or not we are willing to set aside our class prejudices and see people for their character, which is what truly counts. The aspirations of changing social status and social circles are a complicated bit of context throughout the book. But perhaps a related question is how the *source* of good fortune changes our understanding of its *purpose*. What does Abel Magwitch, the former convict and Pip's benefactor, hope for Pip's life? Why was he providing for him?

If we asked what Jesus hoped for in giving His life for us, surely the answer is our own salvation and restoration. Paul said it this way to the Christians in Corinth: "You know the grace of our Lord Jesus Christ. Although he was rich, he became poor for your sakes, so that you could become rich through his poverty" (2 Cor. 8:9).

But salvation was never meant to terminate with us. The riches of God's mercy have been poured out *to* us so that they can go *through* us to the world. This is where the personal dimension of "us" leads to the global dimension. As my mother knew and rightly affirmed about my impetuous insistence as a child that God loved the world and that Jesus came for everyone, recognizing that the gospel is for *you* is just the beginning. Christ came for you so that in you and through you the good news of salvation might come to all. We will have much more to say about that in the chapters ahead.

For now, let the words of Peter's sermon, one of the first sermons ever preached about the good news of Jesus Christ, echo in your ears: "Salvation is found in no one else, for there is no other name under heaven given to mankind by which we must be saved" (Acts 4:12 NIV). With Paul, we can reply, "Thanks be to God, who delivers me through Jesus Christ our Lord!" (Rom. 7:25 NIV).

Tie It Together

For us men and for our salvation
he came down from heaven:
by the power of the Holy Spirit
he became incarnate from the Virgin
Mary, and was made man.
For our sake he was crucified
under Pontius Pilate;
he suffered death and was buried.

What does it mean to believe these words?

- It means knowing that Jesus came for us and that God is for *you.*

- It means believing that this salvation—the putting back together of the world, of all that sin pulled apart—is for *you.*

- It means that from the highest to the lowest, from the powerful to the powerless, there is no one outside the reach of God's salvation. Jesus went to the very bottom and made a way out.

What does it mean to live by these words?

What's a Christian, Anyway?

- It means admitting that we need help.

- It means recognizing that we have sinned, that we have failed to live up to our calling by the things we have done and by the things we have left undone.

- It means confessing that we are under a power, like a virus that has weakened us, and we desperately need the cure. As great as we might think we are, as lousy as we might feel, we are all on level ground. No human can save himself. There is freedom in realizing it, in running into a wall and knowing that you have come to the end of yourself.

Only God can save us.
Thank God for Jesus.

CHAPTER 7

New Beginning in the End

*On the third day he rose again
in accordance with the Scriptures;
he ascended into heaven
and is seated at the right hand of the Father.
He will come again in glory to
judge the living and the dead,
and his kingdom will have no end.*

Interstate 70 in Colorado is the highway to skiers' paradise. It is notoriously crowded on weekends as people try to squeeze in a few days on the slopes to break up the winter blues. I'm not a skier, though it's not for lack of trying. Nor is it for lack of others trying to teach me. Heading downhill at just enough speed to feel not quite in control is not my idea of a good time. Nevertheless, we've made several treks to the mountains to try to introduce our kids to the region's favorite hobby.

For most of the slopes of choice, I-70 is the only real gateway. The most memorable stretch of the drive—whether for the thrill or the terror—is Eisenhower Tunnel, about sixty miles west of Denver. Technically, it's the Johnson Tunnel if you're going east, returning from the slopes, and the Eisenhower Tunnel if you're going west. At a lofty eleven thousand feet above sea level, it is the highest vehicular tunnel in the world. The approximately 1.7-mile stretch is about twenty-six-feet wide for each direction with a height clearance of roughly thirteen feet. No passing is allowed. A recent analysis determined that nearly eleven million vehicles pass through the tunnels each year.[1]

Once you emerge, the scene is breathtaking (and no, that is not a high-altitude, low-oxygen joke). The Rockies tower around you, closer than before in the drive. And that's when what should have been obvious before becomes plain: You've just driven through a mountain. If only Lewis and Clark had lived to see the day.

The first tunnel, Eisenhower, began construction in March 1968 and was completed five years later. The second tunnel began in 1975 and was completed in 1979. Both projects took longer than expected. Harsh winters and fragile rock layers combined to complicate the cause. As one veteran highway engineer quipped, "We were going by the book, but the damned mountain couldn't read."[2]

Nevertheless, it is finished. What was an impasse is now a pass. Where there was an immovable mountain, there is now a highway. You can almost hear echoes of Isaiah: "A voice is crying out: 'Clear the LORD's way in the desert! Make a level highway in the wilderness for our God! Every valley will be raised up, and every mountain and hill will be flattened. Uneven ground will become level, and rough terrain a valley plain'" (Isa. 40:3–4).

The death of Jesus was the ultimate dead end. It was the end of Israel's hopes, the end of the disciples' dreams, the end of a popular movement. Rome thought they had successfully quelled an uprising. Jesus' followers thought their hopes had died. "We had hoped he was the one who would redeem Israel," said one of the early followers of Jesus (Luke 24:21).

The Creed casually states, "On the third day he rose again in accordance with the Scriptures," as though it were simply an expected outcome, as if it were simply a matter of waiting a few days. But that is not how the first followers of Jesus saw it.

The resurrection of Jesus Christ is the most revolutionary event in human history and the most explosive force in the cosmos. Everything is different because God raised Jesus from the dead. Where there was failure, God brought victory. Where there was sin and shame, God poured out forgiveness and redemption. Where there was no way, God made a way. The resurrection is more explosive than dynamite blasting a highway through the Rockies.

NO MORE DEAD ENDS

John's Gospel gives us an up-close and personal view into just how explosive the resurrection is for the dead ends in our lives. After the resurrection, John offered three vignettes of people encountering the risen Christ. John's Gospel is marked by personal encounters with Jesus. Unlike in any of the other Gospels, John gave us snapshots that are deeply personal. Like a movie director who shies away from sweeping action scenes with a huge cast and opts for dialogue, shot in a tight angle, John froze time in his stories to show us Jesus that we might "behold the glory of the only begotten of the Father" (John 1:14, paraphrased). There is Nicodemus and Jesus in John 3, the Samaritan woman in John 4, the woman caught in the act of adultery in John 8, and Mary and Martha as they respond to Lazarus's death in John 11; there is the interaction with Pilate in John 19, and now there are three slowed-down interactions with the post-resurrection Jesus in John 20 and 21.

The first is Mary. This is not the same Mary whom John had already featured—Mary whose sister is Martha and whose brother is Lazarus. No, this is not that Mary. *That* Mary was at Jesus' feet, in tears of grief in John 11 and in worshipful adoration in John 12. *This* Mary is the one from Magdala. This Mary is the one Mark and Luke described as having had seven demons driven out from her (Mark 16:9; Luke 8:2).

However we make sense of that description—an affliction from dark spiritual forces, trauma, physical suffering, mental illness or severe emotional distress, or some combination—we can say with confidence that Mary's life changed dramatically for the better when she first met Jesus. Jesus set her free. Jesus gave her dignity. Jesus gave her a community, a people to belong with, something she may have never experienced before. So when we find Mary grieving at the tomb that Easter morning, she was likely feeling more than the loss of a friend. She was experiencing the complete collapse of a life that she now knew was too good to be true.

Everything had changed for Mary. There was a man who talked about God in a way that she had never heard before, a man who talked to *her* in a way she had never experienced before. There were friends, unlikely friends, who were bound up together in their shared experience of a newfound freedom and joy and hope and peace. And now it was all gone. Once again, *everything* had changed, but this time in a sharply downward direction.

Maybe you can relate to Mary. Maybe you've been let down by Christian leaders or betrayed by a Christian community. Maybe it's deeper than disappointment. Maybe it's disillusionment. Maybe you're even teetering on the edge of despair. Those tears are nearly inconsolable. I say *nearly* because there is one thing that each of us can still cling to, even in the darkest moments: Jesus Christ rose from the dead.

Mary did not know this when this scene opens. John told us that she "stood outside near the tomb" (John 20:11). Crying, she bent down to look into the tomb. When the angels asked her why she was crying, she told them she couldn't find Jesus;

someone had taken Him away and she didn't know where they had put Him.

Don't you feel that way sometimes when you look at how Christianity has been hijacked by people with political or social agendas? Or when pastors or Christian leaders fall or fail or act in wicked ways? It's like someone has taken Jesus away. Like we've lost not just our faith but Jesus Himself.

But the resurrection has something to say about that. The resurrection means that even when the forces of religious corruption and political ambition collude to kill the Son of God, God gets the last word.

And so Jesus, the Word of God, speaks, calling Mary by name. Well, first He addressed her the way she might have seen herself, the way we have been introduced to her in this scene. "Woman, why are you crying?" (John 20:13). She mistook Him for the gardener, which is itself a profoundly theological mistake—Jesus the true and better Adam in the garden on Easter. Jesus in a garden like Eden was a garden—but unlike Eden because Eden was a garden marked by the introduction of death and this is a garden marked by the introduction of resurrection life into the world. Jesus, like Adam (and Eve), was meant to garden the world, bringing forth fruit and life, and who succeeded where Adam failed. The gardener indeed.

But then Jesus called her by her name. He did this because He knew her name. She may not have known where Jesus was, but He knew where she was. She may have lost Him, but He had not lost her. He *knew* her.

Resurrection means grief is not a dead end.

Then there is Thomas. Thomas gets a bad rap, labeled as "doubting Thomas" for saying he would not believe unless he could put his hands in Jesus' wounds. But actually, Thomas was only asking for what the other disciples already had a chance to do. He simply had the poor misfortune of picking the wrong day to miss their dinner club. *Man, the best things happen when I don't show up at small group!*

Thomas was a doubter like we all are doubters. Thomas was a skeptic in the way that any of us would be a skeptic. Maybe Thomas was a little extra salty because he'd been let down before. Maybe his seemingly tough exterior covered a tender wound. Maybe you can relate to Thomas. Have you had a fervent prayer unanswered or ignored? Is there someone you've been asking God to heal or to change or to reach, and it just doesn't seem to matter? Maybe there have been too many promises that have yet to be fulfilled. Whatever the cause, like Thomas, your general approach to Jesus or to the community of faith, we can call it "church" if that helps, is caution or even skepticism.

But the risen Jesus appeared again, this time when Thomas was present. And He came announcing peace. True, deep peace. A peace that settles our souls, that quiets our fears, and soothes our anxieties. Jesus, the risen one, disarms our defenses with the warmth of His presence. He is *here*. And He is here with wounds.

To our skeptical questions, Jesus answers with His scars. To our wrestling hearts struggling with doubt, Jesus gives us His wounds. He *knows*. He's been through it. He bled. He died. He lost. And now He lives.

Resurrection means doubt is not a dead end.

And finally, there is Peter. Peter was supposed to be the leader, the man with the plan, the guy who had the answer to everything. But Peter failed in the moment he should've shined. Like the all-star with the ball in his hands and the game on the line who airballs the shot.

Peter gets painted as a coward, the guy who chickened out when the lights got too bright or the kitchen got too hot. But nothing in John's Gospel gives us that impression. John knew Peter. John told us it was the two of them who had run to the tomb together when they heard that Jesus was alive. Just before the account of Peter's denial is the story of Peter's bravado. Not only had he promised to die with Jesus, but he had drawn his sword and cut off the ear of the high priest's servant, proving his courage and willingness to fight.

I'm not sure fear was the dominant emotion for Peter when a servant girl asked if he knew Jesus. I think Peter was telling the truth when he said that he did not know Jesus. In that moment, he must have felt like he didn't really know Jesus. After all, why had Jesus not fought back? Why, when Peter raised his sword, did Jesus tell him to put it away? Peter had gotten the mission all wrong. Worse yet, Peter had gotten the Messiah all wrong.

Maybe you have too. Maybe you came to Jesus because you thought it would bring an unending string of victories, of blessing and prosperity, of success and ease. And it hasn't. There have been defeats and losses. And you find yourself wondering if you even know this Jesus anymore.

But Jesus found Peter. And He came to renew Peter's love for Him. All was not lost. Jesus is still the one, the one Peter would give his life for, the one Peter really and truly loved.

There is a thread with all three. Mary had lost Jesus. Thomas had missed Jesus. Peter felt he hadn't really known Jesus. And Jesus came to each of them, personally and profoundly, after His resurrection. Because this is what resurrection means: Our grief and our doubts and our failure, our sorrow and our skepticism and our shame cannot keep Jesus from us. No stone can stand in the way. The resurrection is the dynamite of God's love, blasting a highway through it all. God gets the final word: No more dead ends.

ENTHRONEMENT AND EMPOWERMENT

It's easy enough to see the significance of the resurrection, but for many years I thought of the ascension as just sort of a bonus bit in the story, a kind of end-credits scene that was intriguing but not essential. And if you really stop to think about it, it kind of seems like Jesus is just going home like a space explorer returning to earth or, if you prefer, the other way around—an alien going back to its galactic home. Worse still, for some Christians it may provoke feelings of abandonment and emptiness. Jesus is *gone*.

But for all the grief the disciples felt between the cross and the empty tomb, none of that was at the ascension. Why is that? What did they understand that we don't?

When Jesus talked about His ascension, He alluded to a well-known passage from Daniel: "From now on you will see the Son of Man sitting at the right hand of the Mighty One and coming on the clouds of heaven" (Matt. 26:64 NIV). Hearing this, the high priest tore his robes. Jesus was accused of blasphemy, deemed worthy of death. Why? Simply because He made a strange claim to come on the clouds?

Part of our problem is that we read these words of Jesus and immediately think of His second coming, the return of Christ. That's when He will come on the clouds, right? Well, think again. In Daniel 7, Daniel described a vision of the "son of man," a peculiar phrase echoed by Jesus in His declaration.

> In my vision at night I looked, and there before me was one like a son of man, coming with the clouds of heaven. He approached the Ancient of Days and was led into his presence. He was given authority, glory and sovereign power; all nations and peoples of every language worshiped him. His dominion is an everlasting dominion that will not pass away, and his kingdom is one that will never be destroyed. (Dan. 7:13–14 NIV)

For Daniel, the Son of Man was coming on the clouds not down to earth but *up* to the Ancient of Days. More than that, He was going *up* in order to be given glory and power and dominion.

Here is our first revelation about the meaning of Jesus' ascension: The ascension is about Jesus going to the throne.

Jesus is going up to the control room of the cosmos, as it were, taking His rightful place. Far from abandoning us or returning home, He is going to the place where He can do the most good for our world.

But there's more. Paul described the ascension as a vital event that resulted not in an absence but more presence.

This is why it says:

> "When he ascended on high,
> he took many captives
> and gave gifts to his people."

> (What does "he ascended" mean except that he also descended to the lower, earthly regions? He who descended is the very one who ascended higher than all the heavens, in order to fill the whole universe.)
>
> (EPH. 4:8–10 NIV)

The second revelation about the meaning of Jesus' ascension is that the ascension is about Jesus filling the world. He went up in order to *fill* up the cosmos. Paul connected this filling with the giving of the Spirit, a subject we will say much more about in the next chapter. For now, it is enough to reframe our perspective of the ascension from absence to presence.

We are given one more clue in Scripture. This time we look not for shared phrases between the Old and New Testaments, like "son of man," but instead at parallel narrative shapes. The story of the ascension in Acts 1 is quite a bit like the story of Elijah and Elisha in 2 Kings. Here's how that scene goes:

> When the LORD was about to take Elijah up to heaven in a whirlwind, Elijah and Elisha were on their way from Gilgal. . . . When they had crossed, Elijah said to Elisha, "Tell me, what can I do for you before I am taken from you?" "Let me inherit a double portion of your spirit," Elisha replied. "You have asked a difficult thing," Elijah said, "yet if you see me when I am taken from you, it will be yours—otherwise, it will not." As they were walking along and talking together, suddenly a chariot of fire and horses of fire appeared and separated the two of them, and Elijah went up to heaven in a whirlwind. (2 Kings 2:1, 9–11 NIV)

Elisha asked for a double portion of the anointing on Elijah. The sign that he would receive it was if he *saw* Elijah being taking up in the heavens. Now, look at how Luke connected Jesus' promise of empowerment to the ascension. Jesus said to His disciples, "But you will receive power when the Holy Spirit comes on you; and you will be my witnesses in Jerusalem, and in all Judea and Samaria, and to the ends of the earth" (Acts 1:8 NIV). And then Luke wrote, "After he said this, he was taken up before their very eyes, and a cloud hid him from their sight" (Acts 1:9 NIV). The promise of power was followed by the witness of His ascension. This is the third revelation about the meaning of Jesus' ascension:

The ascension is about Jesus empowering His people through the Holy Spirit.

So now we see it: The ascension is not an irrelevant, extraneous detail. Nor is it a reason to feel abandoned. The ascension of Jesus is about His enthronement and our empowerment. Jesus is on the throne! Jesus is filling the universe by the Spirit! Jesus is empowering His church by the Spirit! Now, that's an end-credits scene worth watching.

RETURN AND REIGN

"He will come again in glory to judge the living and the dead, and his kingdom will have no end."

These are the first future-oriented words in the Creed. Up to this point, the Creed has given us statements about God's nature and summaries of what Christ has done. But here are the first words of promise. This is what Jesus *will* do. You have to remember that for the early Christians, their situation was not all that great. Though things were improving by the time the Council of Nicaea was convened, Christians still had vivid memories of suffering and scorn, of rejection and rumors. A different future was something they needed to hold on to. Fixating on the present is a privilege of the comfortable. I think there's much more to explore here, and we will in our chapter on hope. But for now, it's worth sketching an outline of what the early Christians had to say about what God was going to do in the future.

The Creed links Jesus' *return* with His *reign*. He is coming again in glory to judge—hang on. You squirmed, didn't you? To *judge*? Sounds archaic, like an image of an angry, vengeful Jesus. This is one of the places the Christian faith can seem hard to swallow. But to be fair, His followers have not given this aspect of things a great depiction. The way some preachers talk about the return of Jesus, you would think this is God's revenge tour.

Doesn't Revelation give us an image of Jesus riding on a horse with a sword dipped in blood, trampling down armies like grapes in a press? Yes, but there are two central confessions—revelations!—about Jesus that Revelation makes. The first is that He is the first and the last, the Alpha and the Omega. Related to this description is the declaration in Hebrews that Jesus is the same yesterday, today, and forever (Heb. 13:8). This means that the Jesus who is coming again is the *same* Jesus who came down from heaven "for us men and for our salvation." The same Jesus coming to judge is the one who came to die, which leads to the second core image of Jesus in Revelation: He is the Lamb who was slain. Jesus is the one who laid down His own life, who shed His own blood. Could it be that the sword He carries is the symbol of sacrifice, dipped in His own blood?

Nevertheless, judgment is what Jesus will do. Here is where we need a wider lens for judgment. Judgment is not purely *punitive* or even *retributive*. It is more than punishment and payback. Judgment, when God does it, is also *restorative*. In other words, there is a perfect kind of judgment that goes beyond punishment and payback to put all things back together again.

This judgment holds together *justice* and *righteousness,* two words that are almost always paired in the Old Testament. The prophets and psalmists can hardly speak of God's righteousness without also speaking of His justice, and vice versa. Here is one example from Psalm 89:14: "Righteousness and justice are the foundation of your throne; love and faithfulness go before you" (NIV).

Notice the connection not only between righteousness and justice, but between both of those and God's *throne.* Now we see what the early Christians were up to: Christ's *return* is connected to His *reign,* and Christ's *reign* brings about *righteousness* and *justice,* the setting right of all things.

There is one other misconception we make when we imagine the second coming: It's to see it as an evacuation operation. Jesus is coming, so we're getting out of here! Maybe it's not a coincidence that this view became popular in America during the Vietnam War, where American soldiers were being airlifted out of the mess and the danger of the war.

But just as the ascension was not *Jesus'* escape, so His return is not *our* evacuation. The passage that is often quoted to confirm the misconception is from 1 Thessalonians 4:16–17:

This is because the Lord himself will come down from heaven with the signal of a shout by the head angel and a blast on God's trumpet. First, those who are dead in Christ will rise. Then, we who are living and still around will be taken up together with them in the clouds to meet with the Lord in the air. That way we will always be with the Lord.

But as a range of scholars, from N. T. Wright to Richard Middleton to Carmen Imes to Beth Felker Jones, have shown, this is a reference to how Roman citizens went out to meet the visiting Caesar. When Caesar would visit a remote region of the empire, only Roman citizens were allowed to go to meet him. Some citizens were in these other cities because they had fought in Roman wars and been offered retirement anywhere but Rome to avoid crowding. The others—people who had been conquered by war or annexed or assimilated—had some benefits from the empire, but no status as citizens. Those who had the honor of being citizens rushed out of the city to meet "the lord" in order to escort him back into the city as part of his entourage.

And why would Christians be welcoming Jesus to earth? Because this is the ultimate answer to the prayer Jesus taught His disciples to pray: "Your kingdom come, your will be done, on *earth* as it is in heaven" (Matt. 6:10 NIV, emphasis added). In the words of a worship chorus, "When the king comes, so does the kingdom."

Far from being a revenge tour or an evacuation operation, the return of Jesus is about the reign of Jesus that will bring about the restoration of all things. There is so much more to say about all this, and we will when we come to the other line the Creed offers about hope. It is in fact the very last line of the Creed, and it will shape our reflections in a whole chapter on Christian hope.

As we conclude this chapter, my desire is that you will see what the early Christians knew: Because Jesus is coming again, we have hope.

I grew up watching movies about the second coming that were all about a so-called rapture, based on misreading the gospel passages about two people being in a field and one being taken while the other was left behind. (If you read it carefully and think about the destruction of Jerusalem that was to come in AD 70, you will see Jesus offering a prophetic warning about the troubles that would arise for Jews and for Christians. And in that scenario, it was a *good thing* if you had been left behind because it meant you hadn't been captured.) I had no interest in thinking about Jesus' return. It was not a source of hope, let alone joy. It was a cause for fear and dread! Had I done enough to be counted worthy of being raptured? Would I survive a tribulation?

But when you remember that the book of Revelation was written to encourage persecuted and oppressed Christians with a vision of Jesus, you will see that the slain Lamb is the only one worthy to judge with justice and mercy. The one who died for His enemies has the right to wield the sword. Only Jesus can perfectly hold together righteousness and justice, setting the world right and bringing about the end of evil once and for all.

That is a King whose kingdom we never want to end.

Tie It Together

*On the third day he rose again
in accordance with the Scriptures;
he ascended into heaven
and is seated at the right hand of the Father.
He will come again in glory to
judge the living and the dead,
and his kingdom will have no end.*

What does it mean to believe these words?

- It means believing that God loves with a love that is stronger than death. He loves you so much that He won't let anything stand in the way of His mission to save you—not failure, not shame, not disappointment or doubt.

- It means recognizing that because Jesus is seated in victory at the right hand of the Father, you have all the power you need for victory in daily life over the devil's schemes.

- It means being grounded in the hope that one day the "It is finished" of Calvary (John 19:30 NIV) will be the "It is done" of new creation (Rev. 21:6 NIV).

What does it mean to live by these words?

- There's tremendous freedom available to us here and now, beyond worries great and small, when we embrace the truth of Jesus' resurrection and His imminent return to set things right.

- You can live free and light, holding your head up high with your shoulders back. You can go about your life with an unshakable confidence that God will have the final word, over you and over His world.

CHAPTER 8

Giver of Life

We believe in the Holy Spirit,
the Lord, the giver of Life,
who proceeds from the Father and the Son.
With the Father and the Son he
is worshipped and glorified.
He has spoken through the Prophets.

G rowing up, I had an uncle who was a functional alcoholic. I know that may mean different things to people, so let me qualify it a bit. He was a lawyer, respected in his field, and successful by all worldly measures. But at dinner parties, he would drink. And drink. And drink. It was only a matter of time before he would wander over to different guests asking if they had given serious consideration to the fact that *god* spelled backward was *dog* and that perhaps one's dog should be one's actual god. His manner was a toxic mix of glee and aggression, and I remember feeling pretty uncomfortable as a child when he got like that. It was usually our cue to leave.

When my wife and I got married, we went to Malaysia for a second reception, which was actually staged to be much like a second wedding. When it hit me that my drunk uncle would be there, I warned Holly of an inevitable interaction. Sure enough, as the party wore on, my uncle came over to my new bride and asked her if she knew that *god* spelled backward was *dog*, one of his classic lines intended to belittle our family's faith. Sigh. At least she was prepped.

For many people, the Holy Spirit is like the drunk uncle in the Trinity. I say that with my tongue firmly in my cheek and with no blasphemous intent. I mean, we know the Holy Spirit *has* to be at the party; you can't *not* invite Him. And for the most part, things are fine. But there are these moments when the Spirit may just do something that makes us feel uncomfortable—not unsafe and not at risk, but unsettled nevertheless. We want the Spirit to be present; we just don't want Him to make it weird.

I get it. I grew up in a Pentecostal church complete with banners and tambourines and dancers and tongue-talkers. I saw genuine healings *and* I saw people fabricate them. I experienced the power of God in my body and emotions *and* I saw people manipulate crowds toward a collective experience. I grew up knowing the nearness of God *and* wrestling with what that nearness should feel like.

I share this not to boast—how could anyone boast of their roots as if it were their own doing? I share this for two reasons: (1) because I view my growing-up years in the Pentecostal stream as a gift, a gift that for all its shortcomings continues to nudge me toward a deeper and even more experiential life with God through the Spirit, and (2) so that you know I am not talking about the Spirit as an abstraction. So much theological writing about the Spirit is as if the Spirit were a dynamic or an energy or a force. But, as we will explore more in this chapter, the Spirit is a person, the third person of the Trinity, which means the Spirit is not simply something to know *about* but Someone to know.

LORD AND LIFE-GIVER

"We believe in the Holy Spirit, the Lord, the giver of Life . . ."

To call the Holy Spirit "Lord" is to say a few things at once. First, it is a way of communicating that the Spirit is God. Just as Jesus is Lord, so also the Spirit is Lord. Perhaps the choice to use *Lord* for both Jesus and the Spirit, but not for the Father, is a way of highlighting Trinitarian theology.

We already understand that God the Almighty is also Lord. For a religion or set of rituals to be oriented around *a* god would have been normal. And it certainly would have been normal to have had several rituals organized around several different gods concurrently, as was the case in the Roman world. But to identify three as one—to name *two more* as "Lord," assigning the same sovereignty and status to them as to God—would have been groundbreaking.

The relationship between God and Jesus is communicated via the biblical language of Father and Son. The introduction of the Spirit not as energy between Father and Son but as Lord along with the Father and Son expands the worshiper's vision. And in case we are tempted to arrange the three divine Persons in three layers of hierarchy, the early Christians said the Spirit proceeds from the Father. Latin or Roman Christians later expanded this clause to say the Spirit proceeds "from the Father and the Son," an addition the Eastern Church never approved of. But both expressions of the Spirit's procession keep us from seeing the Trinity as a hierarchy, despite the relational distinctions between the Persons. As the early Christian theologians put it, each divine Person shared one essence.

This repeat usage of the *Lord* title is also a cue that the actions of the Trinity cannot be split up. It's not as if the Father does *X*, but the Son does *Y*, and the Spirit does *Z*. No, where one acts, all act. Where one is present, all are present. Theologians refer to this as the "inseparable operations of the Trinity." God in three persons, in perfect unity. This does not mean that each divine person does not have distinctions in their work. Some theologians outline the Trinity as Creator, Redeemer, and Renewer. But we are coming to the limits of language and the bounds of reason. These *distinctions* must not turn into *divisions* in our mind's concept of God. The Trinity cannot be divided.

Michael Bird put it this way:

The divine persons have distinct operations or works appropriate to who they are, that is, the Father is the Creator, the Son is the redeemer, and the Spirit is renewer. But even then, their operations are inseparable, namely, the Father involves the Son and the Spirit in what he does, the Son is the Son of the Father and the bearer and dispenser of the Spirit, and the Spirit is sent by the Father through the Son.[1]

The earliest documents we have from the followers of Jesus are found in the New Testament. Here (in the NIV) the Holy Spirit is referred to as the "Spirit of God" (Rom. 8:9; 15:19; 1 Cor. 2:11; 6:11; 7:40; 12:3; 2 Cor. 3:3; Phil. 3:3) and as the "Spirit of Jesus" (Phil. 1:19).[2] The divinity of the Spirit and the unity of the Trinity are both conveyed in a compact way through the title "Lord."

The Creed goes on to call the Spirit the "giver of Life." Luke Timothy Johnson points out that *giver* is in the present tense. The Spirit is not simply the one who *gave* life; He is the one who *gives* life. This is a significant insight because it overlaps with Paul's language in Ephesians, where he instructed believers to "be filled" with the Spirit. Because the verb is present and continuous, we might say that we are to "go on being filled" with the Spirit. The late New Testament scholar Gordon Fee, whose writings on the Spirit have shaped my thinking profoundly, said it like this:

Paul does not see life in the Spirit as the result of a single experience of the Spirit at the entry point. He simply did

> not have the static view of the Spirit that so many later Christians seem to have. . . . For Paul life in the Spirit begins at conversion; at the same time its experienced dimension is both dynamic and renewable.[3]

The experienced dimension of the Spirit is *dynamic* and *renewable.* Sometimes when we hear the word *filled,* we think of a bucket or a container. The problem with that image is that if a bucket is full, it doesn't need to keep being filled. I heard a friend of mine, Andrew Wilson, a brilliant author and speaker, offer the image of a sail, which resonates very well for me here on the Pacific coast in Southern California. For the boat to keep moving in the water, the sail needs to keep being filled. It's not a one-time event but an ongoing process. That's helpful, isn't it? It certainly captures the renewable element that Fee described.

But still, we must be careful not to think of the Spirit as an impersonal material of some sort, and the word *fill* (whatever image we use) can lead us down that path. Thankfully, infilling language isn't all the New Testament gives us when talking about the Spirit. We are warned against lying to the Spirit (Acts 5), cautioned against grieving the Spirit (Eph. 4:30), and even told to pray in the Spirit (Eph. 6:18). In other words, the Spirit is not a thing that you have or don't have, nor is the Spirit an experience. The Spirit is a *person*! When you think about a person, you get both the renewable and the dynamic. I mean, we all know the difference between a friend we've known for twenty years versus a friend from twenty years ago. A relationship with a person is both *dynamic* and *renewable.*

THE SPIRIT OF SALVATION

As the "giver of Life," the Spirit gives the life of the age to come or what we sometimes call "eternal life." The trouble with the phrase "eternal life" is it makes us think only of a life that does not end. The life on offer, however, is so much more. It's a life of the age to come, a life from the future. This is why Paul called the Spirit a down payment or deposit of the fullness of salvation.

The Spirit's role in salvation is seen from beginning to end. From conviction to revelation, from confession to regeneration, it is the Holy Spirit who gives new life to us. Consider the ways the New Testament describes the ministry and work of the Holy Spirit:

- The Spirit convicts the world of sin (John 16:8–11).
- The Spirit reveals and glorifies Jesus (John 16:12–15).
- The Spirit empowers our confession of Jesus as Lord (1 Cor. 12:3).
- The Spirit gives us new birth (John 3:5–6).
- The Spirit gives us new life and a new status as children of God (Rom. 8:10–11, 14–17).

The first two really stand out to me. How often do I try to be the one to convict someone else of sin? How often do I think my argument or insight will be the tipping point that changes their minds? As good and as helpful as conversations and sermons may be for persuasion, there is only one who can bring true and lasting repentance—the Spirit of God.

And then I think about how only the Holy Spirit can actually reveal Jesus to others. When I was a worship leader, I wanted people to experience the presence of God so badly, to encounter God in personal and powerful ways. At times, it was tempting to arrange songs or create musical moments that could *stimulate*, or dare I say even *manipulate*, a congregation into an experience. But I had to remember, time and time again, that my role was to *facilitate*. Use your gifts; use beauty and art and aesthetics and acoustics, to guide people into the presence of God. Make the conditions favorable to an experience of God. But then take your hands off the wheel. Recognize that only the Holy Spirit can take our words and our music and our art and our gifts and make them something more, something that reveals the wonder of who Jesus is.

Maybe your concern at this moment is that it can sound like we're being passive, like we're shrugging our shoulders and saying, "Oh well. If God wants to reach them, He will." I'm sure some have arrived at such conclusions. But that is not what I'm getting at. I actually think if we realized how crucial the Holy Spirit's role is in preparing and prompting and provoking a person toward faith in Christ, we would become much more passionate about prayer. We would put far less confidence—though not necessarily less effort and attention—in our own work, and devote ourselves, as the early Christians did, to prayer. We are to foster a dependence and even a desperation for God, the kind of desperation you see in the pages of Scripture from those who understood how much this all depends on God.

Unless you go with us, we will not go. (Ex. 33:14–16)

Unless the Lord builds the house, those who build it labor in vain. (Ps. 127:1)

To whom shall we go, Lord? You have the words of life. (John 6:68)

GOD'S POWERFUL PRESENCE

There is more to the life that the Spirit gives. It does not cease after what we might call conversion. That is not where the Spirit's work terminates. Yet for so many Christians, that is where it functionally ends. We speak of the Spirit in the past tense or in a distant sense. But if we are to live like we believe that the Holy Spirit is the Lord—God, the third person of the Trinity—and the giver of Life, then we must welcome not just the work but the presence of the Holy Spirit with us.

Gordon Fee's marvelous descriptive phrase for the Holy Spirit was "God's empowering presence."[4] There are two broad categories in which the powerful presence of God is at work in our lives: to produce fruit and to give gifts.

The Spirit Produces Fruit

Paul, writing to the church in Galatia, instructed them to live out their faith in Christ by the power of the Holy Spirit. "I say be guided by the Spirit and you won't carry out your selfish desires" (Gal. 5:16). The only way to become different is to allow the Spirit to lead you. God's call is never simply *away* from something; His word is not a mere command to stop. It is always a call *toward* something: life. Turn and live, God says.

Without this perspective on the Holy Spirit, discipleship—the process of becoming more like Jesus—can devolve into a list of dos and don'ts. It can quickly become behavioristic and legalistic. This, in fact, is one of Paul's arguments in Galatians about how some Jews had begun to treat their Torah. Given as a gift of God and a sign of grace, the Torah provided instructions about how to live as God's chosen people (not how to *become* God's chosen people). Yet humans have a propensity to twist and taint good things, and the Law had become a reason for boasting (Paul rebuked this strongly in Romans). And obedience to the Law, down to the toughest parts like circumcision, was viewed by some as a kind of badge of honor.

Paul was trying to show them that they were missing the point. Faith was always the central and most important way of responding to God's grace. Faith was how Abraham responded to God's covenantal call, and faith is how we respond to Christ's open door. Jesus fulfilled Israel's commission by opening the way to the Gentiles. Adherence to Jewish law was not a prerequisite for entry; it had been a preamble to the Jesus story.

Sounds like freedom. Yet this does not give us freedom to live as we please. Rather, the freedom we gain in Christ is to be used in service to Christ and to one another. It would be tempting now for new Christians to slip into a simple dualism: Create a new law or live without any codes. This is where

Paul's theology of the Spirit comes into play: "But if you are being led by the Spirit, you aren't under the Law. . . . But the fruit of the Spirit is love, joy, peace, patience, kindness, goodness, faithfulness, gentleness, and self-control. There is no law against things like this" (Gal. 5:18, 22–23).

You want to live free from the law? Be led by the Spirit. You want to stop asking, "Am I allowed to do this?" Let the Spirit produce the fruit of love and joy and peace and more in you and you won't have to worry about what's permissible. The life the Spirit gives is not merely a no; it is also a yes—a yes and amen to all that God promises.

How do we welcome the Spirit's work in our lives? Earlier we referenced the Ephesians text, where we are told to essentially go on being filled. To me, that comes with a portrait of openness, a posture of hunger and desire. But what else *practically* does this look like? In his letter to the Colossians, Paul wrote a nearly identical phrase to the one in Ephesians, but instead of calling us to be filled with the Spirit, he wrote: "The word of Christ must live in you richly. Teach and warn each other with all wisdom by singing psalms, hymns, and spiritual songs. Sing to God with gratitude in your hearts" (Col. 3:16).

Why did Paul do this?

The early Christians went on in the Creed to say that the Holy Spirit "has spoken through the Prophets." This is a way of demonstrating the Spirit's work in what we call the Old Testament. Though there was no conception of a Trinity in the Jewish faith, Paul was pointing back to references to the Spirit of God and saying *that* was the third person of the

Trinity at work. The same God who was speaking through *these* prophets—Peter and Paul and the writers of the New Testament—spoke through *those* prophets, Isaiah and Jeremiah and more. But the term could also be a broad way of referring to Scripture in general. Because it was the Holy Spirit speaking through the prophets and thus also through the word of Christ (the good news about Jesus), to let the word of Christ dwell in your heart *is* to be filled with the Spirit.

Perhaps an illustration can help. When I was a kid, crayon boxes had only about six colors. I thought that was plenty. It never seemed to be insufficient. But when my kids were younger, we would buy them these super sets of sixty-four colors. I had never seen so many shades of blue! But whether they used all of them or not, the more colors you have, the more vibrant your pictures will be. The Bible is like a box of crayons in the hands of the Holy Spirit. The more of it you take in, the more you read and memorize and internalize, the more crayons you are giving the Spirit to work with. And if it is the Spirit's work, as Jesus said it is, to reveal Jesus to us, then don't we want to make the picture as vibrant as possible? The Holy Spirit speaks through what He spoke. *Be filled with the Spirit by letting the Word of God fill you.*

Here is the final link between the Law and the Spirit. The commandments reveal God's character and our calling as His people. But they cannot produce the life we are meant to have. When we rely on them for that, they become bondage. But when we take the words of God into our hearts, seeing Jesus as the fulfillment and center of it all, the Spirit breathes these words of life into us. And what results is fruit that makes our lives look like Christ's. Further, in the Jewish festival of Pentecost, there's a cool (and often overlooked) connection between the commandments and the Spirit: Pentecost was a feast commemorating the giving of the commandments, but in the book of Acts, it became the occasion for the outpouring of the Holy Spirit.

Obviously, much more can be said about how to experience the presence and power of the Spirit on an ongoing basis. Prayer in the various shapes it takes, from contemplative practices to corporate rituals to charismatic expressions, is certainly a key part of the conversation. And the way we come to bear fruit that glorifies God and reveals Jesus is a much more complex subject that many who write on spiritual formation are trying to tackle. But all of that is for a very different kind of book.[5]

Now it is time to turn our attention to the other broad way we see the powerful presence of God at work in us through the Holy Spirit: the giving of gifts.

The Spirit Gives Gifts

The New Testament contains various lists of what have been called "spiritual gifts." Paul used a few different Greek words to describe the way the Spirit shows up in power:

> Now about the gifts of the Spirit, brothers and sisters, I do not want you to be uninformed. . . . There are different kinds of gifts, but the same Spirit distributes them. There

are different kinds of service, but the same Lord. There are different kinds of working, but in all of them and in everyone it is the same God at work. Now to each one the manifestation of the Spirit is given for the common good. (1 Cor. 12:1, 4–7 NIV)

Some of the manifestations of the Spirit are:

- *charism*—gifts
- *diakonia*—service
- *energema*—working

First Corinthians 12 and 14 list several examples of those manifestations. So does Romans 12. Once again, there are some wonderful books that unpack more of what these gifts and services look like in action. For our purposes here, it may be helpful to briefly examine the question of *why* the Spirit gives these gifts.

Let me pause to say that I am using *gifts* to stand in for all the various manifestations of the Spirit's power because it captures something close to the heart of early Christian theology. The word for gift (*charism*) comes from the word for grace (*charis*). We speak often about the grace of God in Christ Jesus, and we do so unashamedly. But when it comes to spiritual gifts, we get embarrassed or squirmy. It's that whole "drunk uncle" thing. So we relegate spiritual gifts to optional extra credit for the hardcore Christians—or the super weird ones. But when we use gift language, we need to see the connection to grace. God the Father pours out His grace. It comes through Jesus the Son and through the Holy Spirit. We would never say no to the grace available to us in Jesus. But how often do we say no to the grace available to us through the Spirit?

Now, I know we cannot divide up the actions or operations of the Trinity, as we said earlier. But this is more about a division in *our* thinking than in the Trinity. It's not about us having more of God but about God having more of us. Open yourself up to all the grace God has lavished on you. *A spiritual gift is the grace of God made visible in and through us.*

Okay, back to the question: Why does the Spirit give gifts? The New Testament records at least three reasons: to build up the church, to witness to the world, and to glorify God.

Paul said the first pretty directly: "So it is with you. Since you are eager for gifts of the Spirit, try to excel in those that build up the church. . . . What then shall we say, brothers and sisters? When you come together, each of you has a hymn, or a word of instruction, a revelation, a tongue or an interpretation. Everything must be done so that the church may be built up" (1 Cor. 14:12, 26 NIV). Gifts are not bragging rights. Nor are they markers of spiritual maturity, a mistake often made in America with celebrity preachers. Gifts are graces given to us for someone else's sake. And usually, it's for the church. This means that holding back on a pursuit of spiritual gifts doesn't just rob you of joy; it robs the church of what God could bring through you. Paul urged the Corinthians to "follow the way of love and eagerly desire gifts of the Spirit" (1 Cor. 14:1 NIV).

This was right after a whole chapter about the revolutionary love revealed in Christ. It is Christlike love that leads us to pursue the Holy Spirit's power.

Second, the Spirit gives gifts to help us witness to the world. I've been part of some remarkable experiences of the presence of God in church and student movements. The temptation is always to scale and sustain what God intends to disperse and deploy. The Spirit is poured out so that the church can be sent out. Later in 1 Corinthians, Paul described a worship service that an unbeliever might attend. If they were to hear them prophesying, proclaiming the revelatory truth of who Jesus is, they would "fall down and worship God, exclaiming, 'God is really among you!'" (1 Cor. 14:25 NIV).

Manifestations of the Spirit are never meant to terminate with us. God doesn't show up to give us goose bumps and then leave. God makes His presence known in and through us so that the world will know and worship Him. In February 2023, a chapel service at Asbury University spilled over into nonstop prayer and worship that kept on going. It attracted fifty thousand visitors from around the nation and many from other nations as well.[6] The 144 hours of "outpouring" sparked remarkable repentance, a focus on holiness, and a genuine commissioning to go and serve others in Jesus' name. At the core of each service was an unhurried adoration of Jesus; beholding Him as the Spirit revealed Him to worshipers without any assistance from renowned speakers or worship leaders.

I've talked to friends who made the pilgrimage, and I've watched a beautiful testimonial documentary from participants who were adamant about redacting their names. One of my favorite things about the Asbury Outpouring is that it ended. Here is what Dr. Kevin Brown, president of the university, wrote about the decision:

> I have been asked if Asbury is "stopping" this outpouring of God's Spirit and the stirring of human hearts. I have responded by pointing out that we cannot stop something we did not start. This was never planned. Over the last few weeks, we have been honored to steward and host services and the guests who have traveled far and wide to attend them. The trajectory of renewal meetings is always outward—and that is beginning to occur.[7]

The outpouring at Pentecost didn't stay in the upper room. Nor did it at Asbury. Nor should it with us. The Spirit moves in us so that the Spirit can move through us for the sake of the world.

The third reason the Spirit gives gifts is to glorify God. Remember the scene Paul described in 1 Corinthians 14? Unbelievers will come in, hear believers prophesying, revealing Jesus in their Spirit-inspired speech, and they will *worship God*. The goal of the gifts is the glory of God. Here we must remind ourselves of the second line in the Creed in the stanza on the Holy Spirit: "With the Father and the Son he is worshiped and glorified." When we glorify God as a result of the operation of the gifts of the Spirit, we are glorifying Father, Son, and Holy Spirit.

WORSHIP AND WELCOME

I have attempted to sketch a bit of a picture of what it would look like to live like we believe in the Spirit as Lord and the giver of Life, as the one who has spoken through the Word of God, as the one to be worshiped and glorified. But maybe you're still a little hesitant. You don't want to make it weird. I understand. Over the course of my life, I have seen some pretty weird things done in the name of a "move of the Spirit."

And yet, I have been profoundly changed by a life in the Spirit. In my high school years, I learned to wake up each morning and pray "Good morning, Holy Spirit" as a simple way of becoming aware of God's presence with me and within me. As an adult, I regularly invite the presence and power of God by praying, "Come, Holy Spirit." This is not some weird fringe prayer. It is one of the oldest prayers of the church.

When early Christians celebrated the Lord's Table, they began to experience the presence of the risen Christ in their midst as they broke bread and drank wine. It was an experience that was in continuity with the story at the end of Luke's Gospel where the disciples on the road to Emmaus encountered Jesus in the breaking of bread. As their theology got worked out, they knew it was the Holy Spirit, the Spirit of Christ, causing them to experience Jesus in the receiving of His body and blood. Over time, as a eucharistic liturgy became more established, there came to be a clear moment when the Spirit's presence was welcomed. In Latin, this prayer is called the *epiclesis*, which is essentially a "Come, Holy Spirit" moment. Later, Christian prayers and hymns would explicitly call on the Spirit to come—*Veni Sancte Spiritus* and *Veni Creator Spiritus* are a couple of examples of that.

Tie It Together

We believe in the Holy Spirit,
the Lord, the giver of Life,
who proceeds from the Father and the Son.
With the Father and the Son he is
worshipped and glorified.
He has spoken through the Prophets.

What does it mean to believe these words?

- It means believing that the Holy Spirit is God and is worthy of our worship.

- It means recognizing the Holy Spirit as God's personal presence with us.

- It means embracing the power of God through the Holy Spirit to work in us to glorify Him, build up the church, and witness to the world.

137

What's a Christian, Anyway?

What does it mean to live by these words?

- It means welcoming the presence of God in your life.

- It means welcoming the power of God to work in your life. Greater intimacy with God is possible. Greater power to build up the church awaits you. Greater capacity to glorify God with your whole life is yours now.

So let's pause for a minute.
Breathe with me.
Slow down for a moment.
Pray with me: Come, Holy Spirit.

CHAPTER 9

An Impossible Dream

We believe in one holy catholic
and apostolic Church.

In one of the many hilarious scenes of the sophomoric comedy *Anchorman*, Will Ferrell's classic character Ron Burgundy reads his name at the news desk on air with a tone of quizzicality. "You stay classy, San Diego. I'm Ron Burgundy?" The camera pans to Ron looking puzzled. The producer then says, "Who typed a question mark on the teleprompter? For the last time, anything you put on that prompter, Burgundy will read!"[1]

We have now come to a few lines in the Creed that we'd rather *not* read, at least not out loud. This is a line in the Creed, perhaps for the first time, when the Christian is most likely to add a question mark. We understand that what we say about the Father, the Son, and the Holy Spirit we should say with confidence and faith. But why should we speak so boldly about the church? How could we possibly say that we *believe* in the church? Believing in God—a perfect, divine, loving Being—is hard enough. But the church? It's a human institution, after all. What place does it have in our confession of faith? For many of us, the idea of the church actually being united and holy seems like an impossible dream.

I get it. I was twenty-eight years old when I found myself standing against the back wall of a crowded room with the entire pastoral staff of a megachurch in Colorado Springs. Up front was a man I had never met but whose name and reputation I was familiar with. He was one of our overseers, a group whose only role was to keep the senior pastor in line theologically and morally. The idea was that other than their personal conversations with the senior pastor and the occasional guest preaching work, the staff would never see these overseers unless something had gone terribly wrong. And today, November 1, 2006, something had gone wrong.

"Well, some of it is true," the man up front drawled in his charming Southern way. "He has been living in sin." I don't know if that's exactly what he said, but it was something to that effect. The rumors that had been swirling that day about a sex and drugs scandal involving the founding senior pastor of our church and a male prostitute were shocking and salacious. Now, a mere twelve hours later, we heard that enough of it was true to warrant his dismissal. I was stunned.

This was a guy who had come in to help *other* churches when *their* pastors had fallen. He was the shepherd of shepherds. In fact, the summer before I moved to Colorado, he had come to help bring calm to a church in Tulsa when their senior pastor had been caught in an affair. I thought moving to Colorado to work for him was a smart move and a safe bet. For six years I had thought how amazing it was to be working for someone so smart, so real, so raw, so different. And yet, here I was standing against the back wall of a crowded room with my colleagues. And there were tears streaming down my face.

Good thing no one asked me then if I believed in the church.

There are serious issues with the church, and we must take these issues seriously. But it will be helpful if we examine what exactly we are saying we believe about the church. There are four key words: *one, holy, catholic* (think: worldwide or global), and *apostolic*. We're going to take one word at a time and look at what it reveals about the nature and calling of the church and then ask what it would take to live into that. When we're done, we'll return to our objection—our protest that springs from weariness or wounding—that we cannot possibly confess a belief in the church.

ONE CHURCH

The Creed was, if nothing else, an instrument of unity. It was designed to clarify and unify the early Christian communities around the core confession of faith. The object of Christian faith is the triune God. Yet this confession, this trust in the Father, Son, and Holy Spirit, binds together the people of God. Just as the first two stanzas of the Creed open with confessions of belief in one God and one Lord, so the third stanza contains a profession of belief in one church. Because there is only one God and only one Lord, there is only one church.

This is a statement; it is a declaration, not an aspiration. We are not trying to become one; we *are* one whether we recognize it or not. In that way, it is rather like a wedding ceremony where the pastor or the priest declares that a man and a woman are now husband and wife, that the two have become one. Anyone who is married or who has been married knows that it will take a lifetime, God willing, to actually become what we already are. It is quite a bit like our Christian lives. In Christ, we are declared righteous; now for the rest of our lives, by the grace of God and the power of the Holy Spirit, we become what we already are. At the wedding you become one, and in a marriage, you become one.

This is exactly how Paul's pastoral logic works in his letter to the Ephesians. Early on he wrote:

Christ is our peace. He made both Jews and Gentiles into one group. With his body, he broke down the barrier of hatred that divided us. . . . He reconciled them both as one body to God by the cross, which ended the hostility to God. (Eph. 2:14, 16)

Jews and Gentiles are one in Christ. Paul expressed the oneness of the church more explicitly a few chapters later:

> You are one body and one spirit, just as God also called you in one hope. There is one Lord, one faith, one baptism, and one God and Father of all, who is over all, through all, and in all. (Eph. 4:4–6)

Some years ago, I was at a conference in London with thousands of church leaders from around the world. Not long before the conference, a group of Coptic Christians in Egypt had just been brutally slaughtered by the Islamic terrorist group ISIS. They had been lined up on the shores of a beach, clothed in orange, and heads covered by sacks, before they were beheaded. It was gruesome and disturbing to say the least. The images and footage had been circulated as part of a campaign of terror and fear. Christians around the world were searching for ways to express solidarity with these Christians.

Nicky Gumbel, one of the speakers at the conference in London—truthfully, he was the convener, but he's too humble to claim that role—shared how important it is to recognize what unites us as Christians. He drove his point home by referring to the Coptic Christian martyrs. No one from ISIS asked what denomination the captured Christians belonged to; no one asked about their views on baptism or the end times. They simply asked if they were followers of Jesus, and if so, the penalty was death, which raises a sobering question: If the evil one, the devil who is behind every opposition against Christ and His church in the world, makes no sharp distinction between denominations or doctrines among Christians, why do we? Why do we let points of distinction become points of division? Why do we forget that the one who unites is stronger than anything that could divide us?

There is only one church.

Practicing Unity

But we cannot just say we are one and call it done. That simply won't do. We must *live* into that unity in order to give that unity visible expression. Paul outlined in his letter to the Ephesians how the church should live in light of the fact that the church is one:

> Conduct yourselves with all humility, gentleness, and patience. Accept each other with love, and make an effort to preserve the unity of the Spirit with the peace that ties you together. (Eph. 4:2–3)

What does "make an effort" look like? Well, Paul the pastor had some thoughts:

> Let all bitterness and wrath and anger and clamor and slander be put away from you, along with all malice. Be kind to one another, tenderhearted, forgiving one another, as God in Christ forgave you. (Eph. 4:31–32 ESV)

I'd like to suggest five practices from this passage to live as one church.

The first is *embrace humility*. Daryl Van Tongeren has a helpful way of talking about humility as "right-sizing yourself." He outlines three aspects of humility: an accurate knowledge of yourself, of your limitations and abilities; a regulated ego; and an openness to others and others-oriented stance.[2] That's a great way to think about humility.

The second practice for unity from Ephesians is to *manage reactivity*. Paul talked about putting aside anger. This reminds me of what we've learned from therapists who tell us that anger is a sign that we're operating out of our "reptile brain," the amygdala. We've got to step back, take a breath, go for a walk, find a way to slow down our bodies so that we don't comment or reply or quote-tweet or bark back in the moment. Patience is better than reactivity. A quick reply is seldom the path of virtue.

The third practice for unity is to *cultivate curiosity*. This is what Van Tongeren is getting at with an openness to others and an others-oriented stance. We could all grow in asking better questions—not the sort of questions that fuel a debate, but the questions that spring from genuine interest and fascination. "Tell me more!"

This leads to the fourth practice: *Engage with empathy*. The Ephesians text describes this as being "tenderhearted." But this takes practice. Practice feeling someone else's pain; practice allowing yourself to be moved by another person. Pete and Geri Scazzero outline a habit they call "incarnational listening," where you leave your own world and enter someone else's.[3] That's a great way of thinking about empathy.

Finally, *seek and give forgiveness.* Paul called us to "forgive one another, in the same way God in Christ forgave you in Christ." It's an echo of Jesus' words: "Freely you have received; freely give" (Matt. 10:8 NIV). The more we drink deeply of God's forgiveness for us in Christ, the more easily we are able to let that forgiveness flow outward to others.

There are whole books on the subject of the church's unity. But I hope this outline of a few practices will help us give visible expression to the spiritual reality of our unity in Christ. There is only one church. God help us live like that's true.

HOLY CHURCH

The only thing as difficult to believe as the unity of the church is the holiness of the church. I mean, if we stretched the limits of plausibility by talking about the oneness of the church amid a reality of lived division, talking about the church's holiness might make you want to chuck this book across the room with disgust. The church is holy? As if.

Even as I write, friends are reeling from news of yet another scandal. Another leader in another church found to be living a lie. Big churches and small churches, Catholic churches and Baptist churches, Christian camp leaders and podcast hosts, worship pastors and youth pastors and senior pastors—no one is immune. The abuse of power and the misuse of authority lie at the heart of the loss of credibility for the church. So, for a book about a credible Christianity, this may be the toughest mountain yet on our journey together.

Let's be honest: At some level, we must admit that the church is not holy. It is broken. It is flawed. It has hurt people and used people and abandoned people. Shepherds have devoured the ones they should have protected. The sound of weeping is heard in Ramah. Children have been hurt. The tears of Jesus over Jerusalem flow now for His church. We have missed our day of visitation. The church has failed.

It was the absolute failure of every institution in Israel in the Old Testament—the priests, the kings, and the prophets—that led God to come and do the job Himself. The Old Testament can be read as a stage-by-stage rise and fall of each of these institutions. Priests arose and were largely faithful in Exodus and Numbers. Think of the zealous acts of holiness from Phinehas son of Eleazar in Numbers 25. But the corruption in the priesthood began with Eli and worsened with his sons in 1 Samuel.

Then came the rise of kings with Saul and then David. Surely Israel would now begin living as the full manifestation of the kingdom of God on earth. But the kings turned from God. We see the clear decline from David to Solomon to Jeroboam, and it gets worse from there with the holy nation fracturing into the Northern and Southern Kingdoms.

The prophets arose to critique and correct the kings.

Elijah and Isaiah and many more. Yet one of the final prophets we meet is Jonah, a prophet so bad at his job that he first refused to accept his mission and then resented the successful outcome of his preaching, frustrated that God showed mercy to Israel's repentant enemies! It's not that there weren't good priests or godly kings or faithful prophets right up until the end of the Old Testament—there were. But the failure of these institutions as a whole becomes unmistakably obvious.

Ezekiel 34 is the story of God pronouncing judgments on the wicked shepherds who had abused and exploited their sheep. God would come as the true King and the Good Shepherd to mend and tend His flock. This is what Jesus was alluding to when He called Himself the Good Shepherd in John 10. Jesus is YHWH coming to His people.

It was Israel's failure then, and the church's failure now, that make us long for the return of the King. Once again, we are waiting for Jesus to come.

And yet. *And yet.* In the face of all that is wrong and evil and wicked, God has made a way for even the church to be saved, to be redeemed. The leaders and people who have misrepresented Jesus and caused harm in God's name will be judged—doubly so, according to Jesus (remember the line about tying a millstone around your neck? Matt. 18:6) and Paul (teachers are doubly accountable) in James 3:1. But the church—the church as the community of the redeemed, the church as the people of God, the church as God's new family of Jews plus Gentiles—the church is *holy.*

Few people in the New Testament lived with this conflicted reality like the church planter and pastor Paul. Paul wrote letters appealing to the church to live worthy of its calling. Look now at his letter to the church in Corinth.

> From Paul, called by God's will to be an apostle of Jesus Christ, and from Sosthenes our brother. To God's church that is in Corinth: To those who have been made holy to God in Christ Jesus, who are called to be God's people. (1 Cor. 1:1–2)

"To those who have been made holy." The cognitive dissonance of this statement will quickly become apparent as you keep reading. A few verses later, Paul wrote, "My brothers and sisters, Chloe's people gave me some information about you, that you're fighting with each other" (1 Cor. 1:11).

And then a few chapters in, our jaws hit the floor. "Everyone has heard that there is sexual immorality among you. This is a type of immorality that isn't even heard of among the Gentiles" (1 Cor. 5:1).

"Holy" is not a grade we earn; it's a status we've been granted. "Holy ones," often translated as *saints* in our Bibles, is one of the New Testament's favorite terms for followers of Jesus. Not disciples. Not Christians. *Saints*.

"Holy" is who we are in Christ. We do not earn it. We certainly do not deserve it. But nonetheless, it is who we are. But, as with our oneness, the journey of spiritual formation is about becoming who we already are.

Holiness in Action

How do we live this confession? If we believe the church is holy, how do we live like it is true? The New Testament is full of pastoral admonishment to churches just like the ones you and I belong to. The journey of transformation is rooted in the reality of God's love for us. It is God's love that made us saints, and it is God's love that roots us in the process of becoming saints.

Back to Ephesians. Paul wrote:

> Therefore, imitate God like dearly loved children. Live your life with love, following the example of Christ, who loved us and gave himself for us. He was a sacrificial offering that smelled sweet to God. (Eph. 5:1–2)

Beautiful, isn't it? Holiness begins by remembering our belovedness. But Paul also said that Jesus is the pattern. From a place of belovedness, we are meant to become imitators of Jesus. How does the church actually live like the *body* of Christ? By living *like* Christ, by living according to the pattern of Jesus' life, a pattern of self-giving love.

In case the Ephesians were to miss what this would mean for their normal patterns of life, Paul went full force:

> Sexual immorality, and any kind of impurity or greed, shouldn't even be mentioned among you, which is right for holy persons. Obscene language, silly talk, or vulgar jokes aren't acceptable for believers. Instead, there should be

thanksgiving. Because you know for sure that persons who are sexually immoral, impure, or greedy—which happens when things become gods—those persons won't inherit the kingdom of Christ and God. (Eph. 5:3–5)

God's love for us is not an excuse to live any way we want. Being declared holy is not a cover for bad behavior; it's the beginning of a new life. And this new life is a life that looks like Jesus. "Holy" is a calling, a calling made possible by the power of the Holy Spirit, which is exactly what Paul got to in the remainder of Ephesians 5.

So let's put it this way: When it comes to living holy lives, God's love is the foundation, Christ's life is the pattern, and the Holy Spirit is the power.

Okay, but what does this look like in action? In a word, *repentance*. Years ago, in a nadir of dissatisfaction with what we sometimes lazily refer to as "the modern American evangelical church"—a shorthand for modern worship, catchy preaching, and smooth programming—Holly and I went to visit a few pastors and priests in my city who were from different Christian traditions. We sat with an Anglican priest (before I became one myself) after the service to ask the meaning of each moment of the liturgy. We worshiped with Presbyterians and their magnificent choir in their historic downtown sanctuary. And we stood with the Greek Orthodox for their two-hour service through the Divine Liturgy, written in the fourth century by John Chrysostom.

That service struck me, and not just because there were no

chairs. There were icons on the walls of notable saints through-out church history, panning from left to right. But there was a notable blank spot at the very end. It was as if the painter had quit before the final installment. But the priest explained to us that it was left open because that is where we come into the story. The story of the church continues. Frighteningly, through us.

There was so much that intrigued me. I wanted a follow-up coffee with the priest. He was kind enough to oblige. I peppered him with all the questions you might imagine being asked by a young ministry leader who was two years removed from an earth-shattering scandal involving a pastor he had looked up to. He answered with all the calm of old Obi-Wan Kenobi. And with his black cassock, gray beard, and long hair held up in a man bun, he kind of looked like him too.

One response has stuck with me all these years. It was the answer he gave to my question about discipleship. "What does discipleship or spiritual formation look like in the Orthodox Church?" I asked, quietly pleased with myself for my thoughtful inquiry. His answer came so quickly I hardly had time to lean back.

"Repentance," he said.

Huh? Repentance? The essence of discipleship, he explained, is a pattern of repeatedly turning away and turning toward, at deeper levels until our very core has changed.

How do we grow in holiness? What does holiness look like in action? It looks like repentance.

When I think about how we could possibly confess our

belief in one *holy* church, I think the only answer must be repentance.

Perhaps instead of a question mark at the end of the sentence, there should be a long pause in the middle.

We believe in one, holy . . .

Pause.

Pause.

Pause.

Then pray the breath prayer the Orthodox often pray: "Lord Jesus Christ, Son of God, have mercy on us, sinners."

Saints in Christ who repent as sinners. There's something to that.

GLOBAL CHURCH

The church I grew up attending in Malaysia was led by a team of lay elders, none of whom wanted to preach. It was born out of a move of the Spirit in a home group of businesspeople. By the time they expanded to take over an old movie theater, the rhythm of having guest speakers every Sunday was well-established. It's all I remember. One week it was an evangelist from Australia; another week it would be a prophet from New Zealand; then a teacher from England; next a pastor from America. And on it went. Sometimes they were remarkable for their profound insight and powerful ministry; other times they were remarkable for their style and strangeness.

My exposure to Christianity, as I shared in the opening

of this book, included the Anglican tradition of my mother's family, the love of Scripture from my parents' Baptist pastor-mentor, and the holy wildness of the Spirit from the Pentecostal-charismatic movements. The many streams flowed as one river in our home. So it was not difficult to learn from ministers from the Western church or the Northern hemisphere. Now, years later, I think it is the church in the global South who has something the rest of the world needs.

When the Creed has us confessing our belief in the church, it declares the church to be "catholic." Now, this may catch some of you off guard, but notice the lowercase *c*. It is not referring to the Roman Catholic Church. It is referring to the ordinary meaning of that Greek word. *Catholic* means "universal" or "worldwide." It is all-encompassing, all-inclusive. It's as if the early Christians were anticipating the question, "Which church belongs to Jesus?" or "Which church is born of the Spirit?" And the answer is, "All of them." If this confession of faith and trust in Father, Son, and Holy Spirit is proclaimed in that congregation, then they are part of the worldwide church, the company of the redeemed, the new community.

It's hard for Americans to keep the global church in mind. From my immigrant perspective—though I've been a citizen for nearly two decades—America is massive. Beyond land mass, the regions are diverse. And the church in America has the tribes to match the vastness of America.

But there's a problem. We can encounter a few different churches or read about a few different church leaders and conclude that we know what the church is like. I can't tell you how many people I've talked with who have become disillusioned with the church because of their particular experiences with a handful of churches or even one singular congregation. That does not invalidate their pain or negate their stories. But it does mean it's not the whole story. Part of saying these lines of the Creed is reminding ourselves that the church is bigger than what we see.

Bill Dogterom is a wise theology professor who attends our church. He's a legend in our community and at Vanguard University where he teaches. He told me over dinner one evening that he opens his lecture on the church by asking his students what's wrong with the church. A lively way to begin a class, I suspect. Then in a true Jedi move, he asks them, "What do you know about the church that Jesus doesn't?" Nothing. There's nothing that we see in the church that Jesus doesn't.

But flipping the question is where the conviction comes. *What does Jesus see in the church that we don't?* What does Jesus see that makes Him love the church? What does Jesus know about the church that we don't?

Here's one thing many American Christians don't know about the church:

In 1900, 18% of the world's Christians lived in Asia, Africa, Latin America and Oceania, according to my research. Today that figure is 67%, and by 2050, it is projected to be 77%. Africa is home to 27% of the world's Christians, the largest share in the world, and by 2050, that figure will likely be 39%. For comparison, the United States and

Canada were home to just 11% of all Christians in the world in 2020 and will likely drop to 8% by 2050.[4]

The average Christian today is a twenty-something African female.

This is why it's difficult to walk away from the whole church—the universal, worldwide church—because we've been hurt by one church. It's so tempting to universalize our experience when what is needed is to experience the universal, global church. It doesn't make our pain go away. Perspective is not automatically healing. But it does change the church we see.

HISTORIC CHURCH

There is one final word—*apostolic*. Here we can be brief. For the Roman Catholic Church, this word means a literal connection via leadership succession to the apostles and specifically to Peter. For everyone else, it means a connection to the apostles via their teaching. To confess the Creed is to conform to the distillation and crystallization of the apostles' teaching, the core doctrines of the New Testament. It just means you can't go rogue and call yourself the church.

In our hyper-individualized context in the West, we tend to distrust institutions and place little value on them. We prioritize the individual over the institutional every time. This creeps into the way we think about church. *I'll do it my way.* If

I don't like how the churches in my community are operating, I'll start my own boutique church. It doesn't matter if it grows; it'll be a product I believe in. The impulse is entrepreneurial, not missional or institutional.

But the only way to cultivate sustainability and scalability, to make something last and grow, is to preserve a movement through an institution. Yet to call the church "apostolic" is not to blindly bless an institution. It is simply to say we did not make this stuff up. And we don't get to play fast and loose with it. Tradition matters. Not the tradition of *expression*, but the tradition of *confession*. The faith does not belong to an individual; the faith belongs to the whole church.

WHOSE CHURCH IS IT?

You can see now how all four words—*one, holy, catholic,* and *apostolic*—actually connect. There is only one church. It is worldwide and all-encompassing of every Christian denomination. It exists because it is tethered to the faith of the early church. One faith-line that spans the centuries and the nations. And it is holy. This one new community is set apart, holy unto the Lord. Yet we are not one or holy, and we forget that we are global and historic. And so we repent. And we confess. These lines in the Creed become petition as much as they are proclamation. That is why the very first mention of sin and forgiveness in the Creed is found in the lines that follow. We will turn our attention there in a moment.

There's just one more thing about the church. We began this chapter by acknowledging how hard it is to say that we believe in a human institution. But what if the church is not a human institution after all? The lines about the church are not in their own stanza; they do not comprise a separate article. They are rolled into the section on the Holy Spirit.

Why?

The day of Pentecost in the book of Acts was the occasion for the promised outpouring of the Holy Spirit. But the outpouring was not for an experience of God's presence alone. It was for the good news about Jesus to be preached and for people to repent and to be saved. It was for the birth of the church. The day of Pentecost is the church's birthday. Now, don't misunderstand this. It's not that the day was the church's birthday and the Spirit was God's birthday gift. It's the other way around. *Because God poured out His Spirit, the church was born.*

The result of God's presence and power arriving in the Holy Spirit was the formation of a new community. I think that means that the Spirit is invested in the life of the church. Remember how we talked about the gifts of the Spirit being for the building up of the church? It makes sense, doesn't it? The Spirit wants to build up the community He birthed. Are you looking for the activity of the Holy Spirit? The Spirit is building the church He birthed. Are you chasing a move of the Spirit? The Spirit is moving in and through the church. There is no church without the Spirit. And the best place to find the Spirit is in and among the church.

This is exactly what Paul said to the Ephesian believers. Having outlined how God tore down the dividing wall between Jews and Gentiles and made one new community, Paul emphasized that this new community is really a household; and this household is housed in a building with Christ as the foundation; but this building is really a temple; and this temple is to be filled with the Holy Spirit.

> As God's household, you are built on the foundation of the apostles and prophets with Christ Jesus himself as the cornerstone. The whole building is joined together in him, and it grows up into a temple that is dedicated to the Lord. Christ is building you into a place where God lives through the Spirit. (Eph. 2:20–22)

Jesus is the foundation of the church. The Spirit is the life-giver who birthed and builds and forms and fills the church.

So are we putting our faith in the church? No. When we say, "We believe in one, holy, catholic, and apostolic church," we are really saying that we believe in Jesus who came for the church, and we believe in the Spirit who gives life to the church. We believe that God is the one who calls the global and historic church both one and holy, and God is the only one who can make it so.

You see, the church is not ultimately a human institution. The church is the Lord's.

Tie It Together

We believe in one holy catholic and apostolic Church.

What does it mean to believe these words?

- It means recognizing that just as there is one God, one Lord, and one Spirit, so there is also only one church, global and historic, stretching across the globe and reaching back to the day of Pentecost.

- It means understanding that the grace of God at work in us through the Holy Spirit allows us to become what we already are: one and holy.

- It means trusting ultimately in Jesus as the head of the church, not in a pastor or leader or denomination or brand.

And what does it mean to live by these words?

We've wrestled with this question throughout the chapter, but we can name the answers again in summary here.

- To live as one church, we must learn, by God's grace, to embrace humility, to manage reactivity, to cultivate curiosity, to engage with empathy, and to seek and give forgiveness.

- To live as a holy church, we must let God's love be the foundation, Christ's life be the pattern, and the Holy Spirit be the power. As saints in Christ, we are free to repent as sinners on the path to holiness.

CHAPTER 10

A New Family

We acknowledge one baptism for
the forgiveness of sins.

When our kids were young, they used to play imaginary games to pass the time. Screentime was minimal, and no one had phones yet. Our oldest, Sophia, living out her birthright as leader of the siblings, would often direct the game. Sometimes they were Olympians diving off couches into the "pool" on our carpet. Other times they were the Pevensie kids off in the Narnian woods on a mission from Aslan.

But the most entertaining scenario may have been when they stayed with my parents while Holly and I were traveling, and they decided to play church. To be fair, it was a Sunday morning, and they decided to have home church instead of going since they couldn't all fit in my parents' car. But the kids quickly took over the service. After a nice time of singing and a short message from Sophia, they decided it was time for baptisms. Naturally the younger two were conscripted by the older two as candidates. Thankfully for my parents, the scene did not involve actual water in the bathtub but a blue towel on the floor, and thus, messes were minimal. The service concluded with a "Communion" with crackers and juice. Holly and I chuckled when we heard about it. We were actually quite proud of their liturgical meticulousness: songs, sermon, and sacraments—not bad for an imaginary game of church.

Baptism is the sign of the new covenant the way circumcision was a sign of the first covenant. Both come at the beginning of life. The circumcised son belonged to a covenant family. In a parallel way, baptism is central to the life of the church because it signifies entry into a new community. If the metaphor for salvation is a new birth, as Jesus described (John 3), and if baptism is meant to mark that birth just as the breaking of waters marks a physical birth, then a new birth means a new family.

Baptism for many American Christians is an individual affair. I can't tell you how many times as a pastor I've had people tell me that they decided to baptize their child at the beach or in their pool or even in the bathtub with a group of close friends and family. There's nothing *wrong* per se; it's a good thing to mark the meeting of grace and faith. And yet, it falls short. One might say there is not enough *right* about it.

Where is the rest of the community, the ones you might not have chosen but to whom you and the newly baptized belong nonetheless? Why was the church robbed of the joy of welcoming a new family member?

Southern California is home to some of the most remarkable mass baptism scenes in recent memory. The Jesus Revolution saw thousands come to Jesus and enter the waters of baptism at Pirate's Cove at Newport Beach not far from where I live. It was a move of God that touched generations. And it reverberates today. Churches in the region still get stirred to band together for mass baptisms on those very shores to symbolize a hunger for God to move again in our day. There's so much to love about it.

Yet there is an undercurrent to this impulse that pulls some people to prize the individual over the institutional. "It's not about a church; it's about Jesus" sounds like a great slogan. It seems on the surface to be about unity and a movement rather than names and denominations. To be clear, unity in Christ *should* be valued over tribal loyalties. That was our subject in the previous chapter. But while following Jesus is deeply personal, it is never individual. It is communal and familial. "It's not about a church; it's about Jesus" sounds right until you recognize that baptism is about *both*. No good parent gives birth and then thinks the job is done, leaving the baby in the hospital nursery and heading home.

To be fair, no one at an evangelistic rally or mass baptism intends to abandon new believers. The hope is always for them to "find a church." It would just be better if we helped people understand baptism as entry *into* the church. The early Christians would not have imagined baptisms being detached from the life of a community. No one is baptized into a solo relationship with Jesus; every Christian is baptized into a family. One popular slogan on baptism T-shirts reads, "I have decided." The emphasis on personal faith is good; the detachment from family and community is a misunderstanding of the nature of baptism.

The Creed does not list baptism randomly. It locates it within the lines about the church. To "believe in" the church is to "acknowledge" one baptism. That is why the Creed talks about baptism in the same breath that it talks about church. We in the West center the individual over the institution, but institutions are what preserve the good that individuals do; institutions are how individuals multiply; institutions are how individuals live beyond themselves into the future. The church is an institution, but not an institution like a corporation. The church is an institution the way a family is an institution. As the renowned church historian Robert Louis Wilken wrote, "Christianity came into the world as a community, not a casual association of individual believers."[1]

REVOLUTIONARY UNITY

The repeat of the word *one* in this line is meant to be a callback to the previous line. We believe in "one . . . Church" because we acknowledge only "one baptism." The Catholics don't have a baptism; the Lutherans don't have a baptism; the charismatics don't have a baptism. *Christians* have a baptism: It is one baptism in Christ, our one Lord.

If we think that sounds radical today, it would have been revolutionary then.

The church was the first multiethnic, multicultural, multistrata community.

You see, there are generally two options in human history for how different groups of people interact. The first is *assimilation*, where the smaller or less powerful group gets absorbed into or becomes like the dominant culture. In an empire, the conquered peoples are given an ultimatum between assimilation and annihilation. The second is *segregation*, where the two groups stay in their own corners. More often in empires, the less powerful group is forced into a corner while the more powerful group remains in the center. Rome had both options in their arsenal as an empire. Sometimes they forced assimilation; sometimes they forced segregation. Either way, they retained domination.

Then came a new kind of community, a ragtag group of women and men who believed that a Jewish rabbi who had been crucified by Rome had been raised to *new* life by God. This man was the true Messiah, the Lord and Savior of the world, not just of Israel. The more they reflected on His life and on His teachings, the more they began to shape a new kind of group, a group for which there had been no precedent. In a world that offered only *assimilation* or *segregation*, the church announced something new: *reconciliation*.

Wilken again underscores the point: "Christianity brought into being a new kind of community, defined not by nation or people or language, but by its worship of the one God as known through Jesus Christ."[2]

Wilken is far from the only scholar to note this remarkable feature of early Christianity. The late professor of New Testament language, literature, and theology Larry Hurtado interpreted Paul's radical claim that "there is neither Jew nor Greek; there is neither slave nor free; nor is there male and female, for you are all one in Christ Jesus" (Gal. 3:28) not as assimilation or the obliteration of other identity markers but as the leveling of the ground. Hurtado pointed out that "there continued to be all these types of believers, identified and often addressed by Paul as such." Rather, what Paul meant was that "these various ethnic, social, and biological categories were no longer to function in a negative manner, as status indicators . . . or as a basis for . . . discrimination among members of the churches he established."[3] Instead, a Christian's primary status was now "in Christ"—and it is baptism that signifies that new reality.

A popular trope today is that Christianity spread beyond Jewish cultures only because it had a little help from the Roman Empire. But long before Constantine, the life and teachings of Jesus were compelling His followers after His ascension to "make disciples of all nations" (Matt 28:19)—every *ethnos*. Hurtado made it explicit that "from well within the first couple of decades, the Jesus-movement become transethnic in composition."[4] In case there is ambiguity about what that means, he went on to say that "from this early point onward, early

Christian religious identity was not tied to one's ethnicity and did not involve a connection to any particular ethnic group."[5]

The most concrete demonstration of this was not simply the stories we have, though we have them from Romans and Christians alike. The earliest and most visible expression of the church as a community of radical reconciliation is a burial ground.

In the early 200s, Christians in Rome shared their resources to buy land on the Via Appia Antica outside the city to create an underground burial chamber. They "commissioned artists to decorate the walls and ceilings with frescoes"; and a "Roman Christian by the name of Callistus, who later became bishop of Rome, oversaw the construction, which today is known as the Catacomb of St. Callistus."[6]

Here's why this was significant. In the ancient world, it was terrifying to die without a proper burial—think of wild beasts, heat, and other hostile factors. But it was difficult to afford a burial site. Many paid dues to be part of a funerary union. Christians decided to offer free burial in the catacombs they constructed.

John Paul Dickson, the Australian church historian and professor at Wheaton, provides more context: "Traditional Roman burial grounds, just like traditional Roman life, usually observed strict boundaries between the classes, separating nobles from the plebs with a wall, fence, or border stones."[7] But this was not the case in the Christian catacombs. One archeologist describes the Christian burial grounds as a "heterogenous mixture of persons of different wealth and status with no distinctively unifying beliefs about the representation of privilege in burial."[8] Unlike Roman society, where even in death you were stratified by class and separated by walls or fences or border stones, the catacombs show young and old, rich and poor, nobles and plebs buried side by side. All believers were equal in the Lord in life and in death. And why shouldn't they be? They had already died with Christ and been raised with Christ in the waters of baptism.

The catacombs *enshrined* the reality that baptism *enacted*: All in Christ are one family. We are baptized into this family. We live together. We die together. We will be raised together.

This was how Christianity began. Hurtado gave us a sketch:

> From earliest years . . . what became Christianity went transethnic and translocal, addressing males and females of all social levels and generating circles of followers who were expected to commit to particular beliefs and behavior from the point of initiation into the young religious movement. Though initially small and insignificant in the first centuries, the movement continued to grow and spread geographically, quickly obtaining a salience and having an impact well beyond its numbers.[9]

Dickson zooms out to help us see it:

> The church had no distinctive ethnic profile, either. It started amongst Semitic peoples (Galilean and Judean

Jews), but within twenty years it was embraced by Indo-Europeans in Asia Minor, Greeks, and Italians. Within two hundred years it had spread amongst Arabs, North Africans, Gauls (the French), the Spanish, and the Celts of Britain. . . . Already by the second century, Christians were making this point in their interactions with the pagan world. A text from AD 150 declares, "we live in both Greek and barbarian cities, as each one's lot was cast, and follow the local customs in dress and food and other aspects of life."[10]

THE BOND OF BAPTISM

Here's a provocative question: If Jesus were launching today in your community, what walls would He tear down? If Paul were to write a letter to your church, what work of reconciliation would he commend? There are plenty of walls to choose from in America: the divisions between ethnicity and culture—black, white, Asian, Hispanic, as a few examples; the division between classes like rich, poor, or the various strata of "middle class"; Republican versus Democrat; American versus not; citizens versus immigrants; and on and on we could go.

Years ago, I had the privilege of spending a few days in the home of Eugene and Jan Peterson. I had been deeply impacted by Eugene's vision of pastoral life but was conflicted about how to integrate it into my ministry context. Eugene spoke of pastoral work as personal and local; he described the pastor's life as defined by the hidden work of prayer, study, and spiritual direction. Everything he said seemed to fly in the face of my life in a megachurch. I wondered if I needed to quit and move to a rural area and become something of a parish priest. When I wrote to Eugene, I shared these conflicted feelings with him, asking if I could come visit. He and Jan were gracious enough to welcome my friend Aaron Stern and me into their home for a few days.

Early into our time together, I asked Eugene if he was aware of how his books had become fodder for an anti-institutional movement within American Christianity. Many Christians, disillusioned and disgruntled with the machinery of church, were opting for backyard Bible studies with bourbon and a cigar. *This is what church really is*, they would say to one another. And it was hard to argue with them. Against the depersonalization of crowded congregations, the authenticity of true community was a welcome change. But I felt something was off. It seemed too tainted by that American impulse to create your own thing, to do your own thing, to go off the beaten path just for the sake of individuality. So I asked Eugene about it. "What would you say to the house church movement that is essentially a gathering of friends around a fire?"

His answer surprised me. I thought he would praise the personal and the local as unmitigated goods. Instead, he was cautious. "I would ask them two things," he said after his characteristically long, uncomfortable pause. "First, what connects them to the apostles? In what way is their faith and practice apostolic?" I readily agreed with this. Too many have wandered into error and false teaching by untethering themselves from the tradition—from the family, from the historic church.

Then he continued: "I would also ask them if there is room for someone they would not have chosen." That stopped me in my tracks. *That's it.* The church holds the tension between belonging and welcoming, between authenticity and hospitality. We go deep with one another while remaining open for others to join. The infection of sin runs so deep that even good things—being personal and local, being close and committed—can be corrupted into exclusion. Our feeling of community can devolve into self-congratulatory connection. *Look at us. We're really being the church.* There can be no such talk among the family of Jesus. There must always be one more chair at the table for the person we didn't think to invite.

As our time with the Petersons went on, the conversation occasionally turned to people whom Eugene disagreed with. Some were friends he had once been close with; others were authors or speakers or pastors whose message he was familiar with. But these were ideologies or philosophies of ministry that he objected to, that he had given his life to counter and even oppose. Yet when we asked, admittedly in a cheeky way, what his thoughts were about so and so, he would pause. An uncomfortably long time. And then he would smile with that sparkle in his eyes and reply, "They are my baptized brother." When we pressed him to explain, he simply said that taking our baptism seriously means taking our family connection seriously. We are brothers and sisters whether we like it or not.

New Testament scholar Nijay Gupta wrote in his

commentary on Galatians that in the "first few decades of faith, those who followed and honored Jesus didn't call themselves 'Christians' yet."[11] And since Paul's letters are some of the earliest documents we have of these communities of Jesus followers, we can see the three terms "they regularly used with each other: 'holy people' [or 'saints'], 'believers', and 'brothers/sisters.'"[12] They were more than a community or a congregation; they were much more than an assembly or a club. They were a family, siblings under one God and Father, baptized into one Lord and filled with one Spirit.

FLAWS IN THE FAMILY

But this family is far from perfect. Baptism doesn't gloss over our flaws and fractures. It doesn't pretend everything is okay. Baptism in Christ is for the *forgiveness* of sins.

Isn't it interesting that the Creed's first mention of sin comes in the section about the church? The early Christians were not unaware of the reality of sin. They knew how sin infects and corrupts, how it divides and disrupts. Earlier, we confessed that Jesus came *for us* and *for our salvation*. Implicit in that confession is our *need* for salvation. But now it becomes explicit: It's our sin that's the problem. It's our sin that created our need for salvation.

Many times over the years, I've had Christians express confusion or concern about the way the Creed words it: "one baptism *for* the forgiveness of sins." Surely, they say, baptism doesn't bring about the forgiveness of sins. Certainly not. The early Christians were trying to set apart baptism into Jesus Christ from other ritual washings in other religious practices. Those ritual washings may promise blessings from regional gods, but there is only one baptism that is connected to true and actual forgiveness. It is the baptism into Jesus Christ because Jesus is the one who came for us and for our salvation.

Baptism is how this salvation becomes visible. A sacrament is a visible expression of an invisible grace. As one of the early sacraments of the church, baptism gave physical expression to the faith and grace that come together in salvation. Entering the waters is an act of faith; emerging from the waters is a sign of grace. Earlier, we spoke of baptism as being like passing through the waters of a new birth. In one of the New Testament's other metaphors for baptism, we discover that it is like death and resurrection.

> "Or don't you know that all who were baptized into Christ Jesus were baptized into his death? Therefore, we were buried together with him through baptism into his death, so that just as Christ was raised from the dead through the glory of the Father, we too can walk in newness of life. If we were united together in a death like his, we will also be united together in a resurrection like his." (Rom. 6:3–5)

Going into the waters is a type of death—an old life is dying. Faith is death. To believe in God is to die; it is to rid ourselves of other rivals, to climb off the throne of our own heart and onto the cross. Taking a step of faith is taking up our cross. But resurrection is not something we do. Resurrection is what God does. Coming out of the waters is a sign of God's grace bringing about new life. Like a new birth, resurrection is the work of God to bring about surprising newness.

I'm not sure it is helpful to split apart the faith and grace at play in baptism by speaking of one in the immersion and the other in the emergence, though. Faith and grace are not equal pairs in the salvation story. We are saved by grace through faith, the faithfulness of Christ that we access by our own participation of faith. Yet we must not mistake the power: The main character is God, not us. This is why that church baptism T-shirt slogan "I have decided" misses the mark. It's not simply that it fails to recognize the communal component. It's also that it places the em-PHA-sis on the wrong syl-LA-ble. Ultimately, these lines about baptism are included along with the lines about the church *in that section about the Holy Spirit.*

Baptism doesn't forgive our sins; Jesus does. Baptism does not make us one or make us holy; Jesus does. And Jesus does so through the Holy Spirit. The Spirit gave birth to the church; the Spirit binds the church together; and the Spirit builds the church up.

BUILD MY CHURCH

When God's forgiveness is the headline, we can see the through line of grace in each other's stories. I know this isn't easy. There will likely be many relationships between individuals, between churches, and even between denominations that will be fractured beyond repair on this side of kingdom come. But even if we were to accept some of these breaks in relationships because of the hardness of hearts or out of the need to protect our hearts with wise boundaries, that does not mean we forsake the family altogether.

In the 1200s, a young man named Francesco Bernadone, disillusioned by war and battle, rejected the family business and took to wandering the countryside surrounding his hometown of Assisi in the hills of Umbria. He came upon a little church in need of repair, called San Damiano. He felt drawn to go inside. He knelt before a large wooden crucifix, and the eyes of Jesus seemed to lock in on him. He couldn't look away as feelings of doubt and fear, guilt and desire welled up within him. "Lord, what do You want me to do?" he asked. "Show me what You want me to do with my life."

Jesus replied, "Francis, go and rebuild My church which, as you see, is falling down." Francis began by literally rebuilding that church and a few others in the area. But then he realized the call of Jesus was bigger than that. He founded an order with the pope's blessing that would focus on preaching and serving the poor.

For eight hundred years, Franciscans have been active in the work of foreign missions, including the establishment of numerous missions in the 1700s in California and Mexico. They have also made many contributions to the field of education and scholarship, and the order has contributed six popes to the church. Today, there are about 350,000 Franciscans worldwide. Aren't you glad Francis didn't give up on the church?

Tie It Together

We acknowledge one baptism for
the forgiveness of sins.

What does it mean to believe these words?

- It means recognizing that Christianity is a community, not a collection of individuals.

- It means embracing our bond with one another.

- It means making our confession of belief in the church meaningfully and taking our baptism seriously.

What does it mean to live by these words?

- It means making room for others, especially those whom we would not have chosen.

- It may mean refraining from talking about others on social media as though we'd rather not be associated with them. We can't "other" another Christian. We are bound up with each other.

- It does not mean ignoring the flaws in the family. Sin is part of the story—for now. And yet, when the church doesn't look like the person or actions of Jesus, we don't have to walk away from Jesus. Instead, in whatever feeble and faithful way, we can join Jesus by the power of the Holy Spirit in rebuilding the church.

CHAPTER 11

A More Beautiful Hope

We look for the resurrection of the dead,
and the life of the world to come.

R obert's funeral was the second funeral I had observed in two days. The service took place in a funeral home, an increasingly likely setting for funerals. Located in an industrial complex in a lower income area, the building was religiously neutral, outside and within. I sat at the back of the room, with no one beside me, conspicuously overdressed in my suit. The family procession moved down the aisle with family members wearing baseball caps, likely an homage to Robert.

I was there not as a pastor but as a researcher. One of my

181

projects en route to conducting my actual research for my doctoral dissertation was to get my feet wet in the field of ethnography. Putting qualitative research in "conversation" with theological reflection is a core component of the doctoral research model at Durham University in the UK, but ethnographic work was new to me. Since my larger research would be about hope, I decided to do a small-scale project on evangelical funeral sermons.

We've all heard the lines: Your loved one was a bird in a cage, and death has set her free. Or God needed another angel. Or one of my favorites, he was a pilot and now he's soaring free. Fortunately, the sermons I studied did far better than that.

Robert's sister was emotional during her welcome. She expressed gratitude that her brother knew Jesus and that his struggles were now over and that he was whole. Yet in her prayer that followed, she referred to his death as tragic. A few Scriptures were read. The first was Proverbs 3:5–6, affirming God's sovereign care for our lives. This was followed by a slideshow and a speaker who read a written eulogy. There was an opportunity for people to share their favorite stories of Robert. Though we were in a funeral home, this was clearly a service commemorating a life.

Then, Pastor Mike took the pulpit. He later told me that he is always the last person to speak at a funeral because he likes to take notes on what has been said and weave it in, making the funeral sermon a dynamic thing.

"I was just thinking as I sat there . . . Jamie, and then Miss Bridgette, and now Robert. I feel, quite frankly, like I'm a member of the Ponder family," he began. He was referring, I think, to the funerals of different family members he had done. Pastor Mike is something of a legend at his church—the go-to guy for funerals. He continued. "You can just call me a brother from another mother." Laughter erupted since Pastor Mike, as an African American, was the only non-white person in the room (besides me). This was as loud as they had been all morning.

Pastor Mike continued by reflecting on the major themes of Robert's life. Robert had been through an addiction recovery program, but Pastor Mike was quick to add, "There are none of us here that are perfect and none of us who haven't made mistakes and don't have things we're dealing with right now."

The point was that Robert got help and then offered help to others. Robert, Pastor Mike made clear, was the kind of guy who said by his actions, "I love ya, and I'll go through a wall for you . . . if you are a friend of mine, there's no limit to what I wouldn't do to help you." Pastor Mike had struck a nerve: the longing for belonging, the desire to be loved permanently and unconditionally. Then the sermon began to shift. "We'll miss his smile, we'll miss the jokes . . . but I'm here to tell you, by the Word of God, what God wants to do on your behalf as we deal with this untimely loss."

In our interview after the funeral, Pastor Mike explained that he structures every funeral sermon in three parts: reflection, comfort, and projection. Reflection is about remembering their life, while comfort is "the comfort of the

Scriptures." Projection, in Pastor Mike's words, is simply asking, "If this were you, where would you be?" This closely resembles the famous Billy Graham line that led to his decision moments: "If you died tonight, do you know where you're going?"

As Pastor Mike made the shift into the comfort section in his sermon, he began reading Revelation 21 (NKJV), a familiar passage about a future hope. He paused to give particular emphasis to verse 6, which ends with God's promise to give "the fountain of the water of life freely to him who thirsts."

The sermon began building toward the decision moment. "In each of us, there is a thirst . . ." He began to evoke a revivalist style. "Robert . . . was a giver. He didn't just take but he gave. And that reminds me of a passage that probably everybody in here knows . . . that 'God so loved the world that he'"—emphatically now— "'gave His only begotten Son that whosoever believed on Him should not perish but have everlasting life.'" Pastor Mike drove the point home: "So, what is the lesson for us today? The lesson for us today is that . . ." and here he emphasized each word:

> We. Also. Be. Givers. But you gotta recognize that in order to be a giver you must have a source whereby you receive, and that resource must be God. That resource should be what Jesus Christ did on Calvary, where He suffered and died for your salvation and mine—for Robert's salvation— and for the salvation of everyone who would believe on Him.

Pastor Mike began to leverage Robert's life to call people to Jesus. "Robert totally relied upon what Jesus Christ did on the cross for him. And I believe, if he could speak today . . . he would encourage everyone here to do the same."

Yet Pastor Mike did not make an altar call. Instead, he closed with a charge to live as a giver, just as Robert had done. "But I tell you what, if you will take what [Robert] gave, and the legacy that he left, and allow yourself to emulate that, then when someone stands up here or wherever to talk about your life, they will talk about you as a giver . . . and not just a taker. Amen?"

It was an emotional funeral, and the truth is, it was hard for me to take notes. I relied on my recording of the service later. Death is difficult. But that is why hope is not optional. Hope is a necessity. We need to know "What comes after *this*?"

My small-scale research on evangelical funeral sermons concluded: When evangelicals seek to give hope, they speak of Christ above all. It is not only the *transcendency* of Christ that defines evangelical funeral preaching but also the *immediacy* of Christ's presence. It surprised me to note that there was very little future-orientation, odd since hope is forward facing. This lack of a future-orientation meant the lack of reference to a future bodily resurrection, something the early Christians desperately clung to. In a way, the sermons I studied came close to what theologians call an "over-realized eschatology," an overemphasis on a hope that is already here, treating future promises like present realities. Still, when evangelicals speak of hope, they speak of Jesus and His presence, right here and right now. And that is a good thing.

The question is, *Is it good enough?* Is there a more beautiful hope?

THE HOPE OF THE EARLY CHURCH

I studied funeral sermons as a warm-up to my actual research on hope, in which I studied worship songs of hope (more on that to come). But first I had to study the hope of the early church.

In the first few hundred years of Christianity, the church was growing quickly, and it was spreading to several different regions. A diversity of perspectives shaped various "expectations for the future of the planet and individual, saint and sinner," which could be described as "many facets of a rapidly developing, increasingly detailed Christian view of human destiny, of many hopes—and many fears—enveloped within a single, growing, ever more complex tradition of early Christian faith and practice."[1]

Yet there are some discernible common threads that together form a tapestry of early Christian hope. The first thread is a *linear view of history*. While some might have seen human history as a circle of events that repeats and time itself as cyclical, Christians acknowledge the rhythms of seasons while holding on to a conviction that history has both an origin and an end point. To confess faith in a singular, sovereign God is to place confidence in His purposes, plan, and power for the created world. Just as God the Father is the Creator through the word of the Son and by the life-giving work of the Spirit, so God will be the "pioneer and perfecter" (Heb. 12:2). Just as there was a beginning, so there will be an ending.

A second common thread is a belief in the *future resurrection of the body for believers.* This can be seen as early as second-century apologists up to church leaders like Gregory of Nyssa and Augustine in the fourth and fifth centuries.

> Early Christian theologians insisted on taking the biblical promise of resurrection literally. Christopher Hall outlines in his work on the theology of the church fathers, [that] many of these writers, particularly Athenagoras and Augustine, went to great lengths to show how God could take decomposed and even digested remains of a human and reconstitute them in an act of new creation to bring resurrection about. The body, because it was created by God, will be redeemed by God.[2]

Third, there was a common hope for a *future judgment.* This judgment was thought to be pronounced at the moment of death, though there might be some lag between the pronouncement and the actual experience of either reward or retribution. Though the timeline was fuzzy, "early Christian writers almost universally assumed that the final state of human existence, after God's judgment, will be permanent and perfect happiness for the good, and permanent, all-consuming misery for the wicked."[3]

It is worth saying here that the modern notion of "hell," with flames of torture, derives more from a medieval imagination, like Dante's, than from Scripture. In fact, some evangelicals have argued for either *annihilation*, the view that the "second death" spoken of in the book of Revelation is the end of existence with total and complete finality, or *conditional immortality*, the view that since the New Testament speaks of God as the only eternal one, only those who are in the Lord share in *His* eternal life. Both of these views are orthodox, biblically based alternatives to the inherited view from the medieval church of *eternal conscious torment*. Nevertheless, the early Christians did not define or at least did not agree in their picture of final judgment. But they did not sway from their belief in it. There will be a reckoning to come.

Maybe I need to pause here to explain why judgment is included under the banner of hope. If we're honest, this feels more like something to dread. And yet, justice and judgment are two sides of the same coin. If we are to see things set right, then wrongs must be dealt with. The early Christians, persecuted and marginalized as they were, longed for a day when God would bring about a great reversal, bringing the proud and lofty down and lifting the humble and lowly up. One of the earliest Christian songs, based on Mary's response to learning she would give birth to Jesus, is about precisely this hope (Luke 1:46–55).

Back to the common threads. The fourth and final common thread in the hope of the early church was the belief in the *communion of the saints*. Augustine would give the fullest vision of this in *City of God*. But earlier Christian theologians seemed to have a general sense that Christians who had died were still somehow involved in the life of the church through prayer. The details of how are controversial and disputed. Yet the larger picture to keep in mind is that salvation was thought of in ways that are both communal and ecclesial—the church includes those living on earth and those worshiping in heaven.

The hope of the early church is codified in two lines of the Nicene Creed:

> He [Jesus] will come again in glory to judge the living and the dead.

> We look for the resurrection of the dead . . . and the life of the world to come.

These two phrases taken together provide a summation of early Christian hope. "The Creed confesses a future-oriented hope for the return of Christ, the full reign of Christ, the final judgment of the human race, the resurrection of the believer, and the new creation."[4]

Let's turn now to this final sentence of the Creed and explore it phrase by phrase.

"WE LOOK . . ."

The first and most obvious thing to note here has to do with our posture. The early Christians were *looking*. This is an echo of the language of Romans 8, where Paul spoke of creation waiting "breathless with anticipation" (v. 19) for the children of God to be revealed in resurrected bodies. The slavery of sin that all creation has been subjected to will be broken when the redemption of humans is complete. Some commentators have noted the strangeness of the word Paul chose to express the eager anticipation of creation and have suggested an image of creation on tiptoes, craning its neck as if to see on a far-off horizon or around the corner. The early Christians may have been drawing from that image to shape the posture of their hearts. *We want to look, to stand on edge, to crane our necks, and turn our heads. We're waiting!*

And why wouldn't they? They were not living their best lives. They were experiencing scorn and derision and, in some cases, persecution and death. They had to look to the future because the present was not good.

Hope is incurably future focused.

A funny thing happened when I was researching hope. Part of my focus was on how hope is expressed in contemporary worship songs. But when I surveyed a group of one thousand worship leaders in the United States, I encountered a different conception of hope. I asked the worship leaders to name songs that have brought them hope personally. Later in the survey, I also asked them to name a song that has brought their church hope in a time of despair.

I consolidated the answers to these two questions and tallied up the mentions of songs. Then I took a closer look at the nine most named songs.[5] I looked at the imagery. And I analyzed—this is super nerdy—the verb tenses. In full geek mode, I examined the verb tenses related to divine action (what we sing about God) and the verb tenses related to human action (what we sing about ourselves). I won't bore you with the specific percentages and ratios—I've written on that elsewhere in my academic book *Worship and the World to Come.* But here's the summary: 59 percent of the verbs about God are present tense; 24 percent are about God's actions in the past; and a mere 17 percent are future tense verbs.[6]

The past tense is understandable: We look back at creation or at the cross and resurrection. But why is God's action in the present getting more attention than what God has done and what He will do in the future *combined*? If this were an analysis of a simple list of current popular worship songs, that would not have caught my attention. The fact that these were qualified as *songs of hope* and yet were not about God's actions in the future made me ask some deeper questions.

How could a focus on the present provoke hope? One answer could be that the analysis is flawed because verbs about who God *is* are present tense verbs: You *are* holy, You *are* good, and so on. But another possibility should at least be considered. It could be that the conditions for most modern worship songwriters are pretty comfortable. Relative to other contexts around the world or even compared to the church in other eras, Christians in America, the UK, and Australia—where many of these songwriters live—enjoy freedom of religion and even significant financial benefit from being Christian songwriters. I don't begrudge this. I myself am a beneficiary of this. But the point I'm making is simply this: What if a preoccupation with the present tense is proof of a certain kind of privilege? What if we don't need to look to the future because the present is so good? What if comfort inoculates us from needing a future-oriented hope?

This is in stark contrast to how James Cone described the spirituals from African American slaves in the pre–Civil War era. He argued that the spirituals were about an "eschatological freedom grounded in the events of the historical present, affirming that even now God's future is inconsistent with the realities of slavery."[7] They had what Cone called an "apocalyptic imagination" of a future reality that could not be contained in the present. The future was when liberation would come in fullness; the future was when *Christ* would come in glory to bring about judgment and justice. For the slave whose present condition was full of suffering and oppression, they had to be future-oriented if they were to experience hope in the present.

How can we recover this sense of *looking*, of longing for something beyond this moment? For some American Christians, there might be a tendency to exaggerate the hostility of culture and then reinterpret it as persecution. But that surely cannot be the answer. It would be an insult to the underground church in Iran and China and around the world. To do so would cheapen the blood of the martyrs. I think what is needed for the church in the West is to develop an awareness of the plight of our brothers and sisters around the world in order to demonstrate solidarity with them. We confess that

"We look . . ." the same way that we pray for daily bread: with others in mind. This is a communal "we," a "we" that spans church history and stretches around the globe.

In a 2024 report, "365 million Christians" were living "in nations with high levels of persecution or discrimination." For reference, that's "1 in 7 Christians worldwide, including 1 in 5 believers in Africa, 2 in 5 in Asia, and 1 in 16 in Latin America."[8] North Korea, Somalia, Libya, Eritrea, Yemen, Nigeria, Pakistan, Sudan, Iran, Afghanistan, and India are some of the fifty countries where persecution scores register as "very high" on a matrix of eighty questions. "Almost 5,000 Christians were killed for their faith last year. Almost 4,000 were abducted. Nearly 15,000 churches were attacked or closed. And more than 295,000 Christians were forcibly displaced from their homes because of their faith."[9]

These are our sisters and brothers. They are part of the "We" in the confession of hope in the Creed. *We look . . .*

". . . FOR THE RESURRECTION OF THE DEAD . . ."

So now the question is, What are we looking *for*?

The early Christians named our hope as "the resurrection of the dead." Many Christians might think the only resurrection we believe in is Jesus'. After all, we're going to heaven when we die, and that's it, right?

That's not how centuries of Christians described their hope. They used the word *resurrection* deliberately. It is the word to describe what happened to Jesus. Their firm belief was that God would do for all who are in Christ what God did for Jesus on that very first Easter. Think for a moment about what resurrection is *not*.

Resurrection is *not* the reversal of death. That would be *resuscitation,* something akin to what Lazarus experienced, a kind of coming back from the dead. That means resurrection is also not a return to Eden. We are not going back to anything. We are going forward into something new. More on that in a moment.

Resurrection is *not* passing through death. That is what the Greeks believed: We have an immortal soul that continues in some sense *beyond* death but not a *bodily life after death.* The Romans thought some of their emperors, beginning with Julius Caesar, became a divine soul after their death. But that, as we saw earlier, is not what the early Christians said about Jesus. Remember the stories in the Gospels about Jesus appearing in locked rooms? Those stories taken alone might have led some to believe that Jesus was a spirit or a ghost. That's why the followers of Jesus were sure to also say that He ate and drank and had flesh and blood and scars that they could see and touch. Jesus did not simply pass through death into a sort of spiritual existence.

Similarly, resurrection is also *not* an escape from this life. It is not God's way of airlifting us out of a quagmire of trouble. The disciples found an empty tomb, not a vacated body. They saw a body that had been glorified. Some things about that body were the same, and some things were very different.

Finally, resurrection is *not* progress. Resurrection does not emerge from possibilities that are latent in a corpse. Nobody says at a funeral what potential the deceased has. Death has a finality to it that we understand at our core. Death says, "It is over." Resurrection says, "No." Or to paraphrase the theologian Karl Barth, resurrection is God's "yes" to life and creation. It is God refusing to let go of what He made. Christians do not place their hope in the progress of humanity or in the eventual triumph of society. We do not envision history in an inexorable upward line. We see a break in the line: God breaks in!

So what *is* resurrection? Resurrection is the defeat of death. Resurrection is a word from beyond, a word from the Creator and Life-Giver who speaks to our ending and creates a beginning. Resurrection is the death of death, as one early Christian hymn put it.[10] All that corrupts and decays and destroys God's good world is no more. That which happened to Jesus will now happen for those who are in Him. That's something to *look* for, isn't it?

"... AND THE LIFE OF THE WORLD TO COME."

But the Creed does not stop there. The early Christians went on to say they were also looking for the "life of the world to come."

The "world to come" is a way of saying that we are not going back to Eden, as I mentioned before. The world to come is not a return or a restoration; it is the completion and perfection of creation. The world to come is the world that was, as it was meant to become. That is why John's vision of the new heaven and the new earth in the book of Revelation was not of a garden, as it was in Eden, but rather a garden city. We aren't going back. We're going into the future that was in God's mind at the very beginning of time.

But there's another layer to this. The word for *world* in the Creed's original Greek is better translated as *age*, an *eon*. There is an age to come. Jesus spoke of this often. The early Christians, as seen in the writings of the New Testament, saw the age to come as something that had begun with the resurrection of Jesus. A new day had dawned. And yet, the "present evil age" remained (Gal. 1:4). That means all Christians alive right now are living between the ages, in a long twilight of sorts.

Or as I like to say, we are from the future. Sounds more fun doesn't it? That's what Paul essentially was saying to the church in Ephesus: "You were once darkness, but now you are light in the Lord, so live your life as children of light" (5:8). The light belongs to the new day that has dawned, and the behaviors that belong to it are "every sort of goodness, justice, and truth" (v. 9). Paul warned them not to even "participate in the unfruitful actions of darkness" (v. 11). He drove the point home by quoting from a few different places in Isaiah: "Therefore, it says, *Wake up, sleeper! Get up from the dead, and Christ will shine on you*" (v. 14).

It's a little bit like flying international. Because I grew up in Malaysia, moved to the States, moved back to Malaysia, and then came back to America to go to college, I've had loads of reasons to fly across the Pacific Ocean. I think I've done it twenty-five times. Add that to my cross-Atlantic trips when I was doing my doctoral work in Durham, and I think my transoceanic flights number well over fifty trips. You would think I'd have figured out how to conquer jet lag ages ago. It was only recently that I came across some research about how to reset your body clock more quickly. The key? Mealtimes.

In a 2023 study published by Northwestern University, researchers found that aligning mealtimes with the destination's time zone could help reset the body's internal clock. For instance, if I were flying from Denver to London in the evening, as I have done several times, I should opt for a light dinner and refrain from eating during the flight. Then, upon landing in London, I can indulge in a hearty full English breakfast. This approach, coupled with intentional exposure to bright daylight, was shown to reduce the usual six-day recovery period by up to a third. In other words, you should eat according to the time zone you're going to, not the one you're coming from.

Now that will preach.

All who are in Christ belong to the future that God is bringing. We belong to a different time zone. By the power of the Spirit, we are to live now as it will be then. We need to adjust our appetites to the time zone we are going to rather than the one we are coming from. This explains why Christians have such a different vision of ethics and morality, of justice and righteousness, of love and mercy, and more. We are from the future.

HOPE IS . . .

In my research on hope, I drew from several different models of hope—from the psychological to the philosophical to the theological—to construct a meta model of hope shaped by seven facets. They are the

- *act* of hoping
- *grounds* or basis for hope
- *object* of hope or the thing we are hoping for
- *agent* of hope or the one who will bring it about
- *time* of fulfillment, meaning when the thing hoped for will come about
- *space* of fulfillment, meaning the location where the thing hoped for will arrive
- *pathway* of fulfillment or the means by which the thing hoped for will take place

Based on that framework, my summary of Christian hope is as follows:

Christian hope is a confident assurance (act), grounded in God's promise and faithfulness as revealed in the Scriptures in general and in Christ in particular (grounds), that the triune God (agency) will bring about the "resurrection of the dead and the life of the world to come" (object) at Christ's appearing (time), making heaven and earth new and one (space), by means of what has already been accomplished at the resurrection of Jesus (pathway).[11]

ONE MORE FUNERAL SERMON

I've had the sober honor of preaching at a lot of funerals as a local church pastor. I've missed the mark more than a few times. I've tried to say too much, and I've not said enough. I've given too long an explanation about resurrection hope, and I've also failed to give a sketch of Christian hope at all. I remember all the precious saints whose lives we were honoring. A handful were tragic: a car accident, a sudden heart attack, a child with a terminal illness.

My text is often from John 11, where Jesus met the grieving sisters of Lazarus. Both insisted that if Jesus had been there, their brother would not have died. When Martha came with questions about resurrection, Jesus engaged with her and ultimately pointed to Himself as resurrection in the flesh. When Mary collapsed in a puddle of tears, Jesus wept with her. To both of the sisters, Jesus offered Himself. The story moves me every time I hear it.

But a few years ago, I decided to take a different approach. The funeral was one of the saddest I had ever been part of. A young couple whose premarital counseling I had done and whose wedding I had officiated were pregnant with their first child. Weeks before she came to term, they learned that something was wrong. The baby died shortly after being born. It was gut-wrenching. They opted to do a graveside service instead of a full memorial service at the church. It was a short turnaround, and I had to come up with words that could comfort and be memorable but not too long. After all, we would be outside—in Colorado, in the winter.

And then it hit me. My job is to give voice to the ache we all feel. I began by saying, "It should not be this way." This is not how God made His world to be. This was never part of the design; it is incongruent with the Creator's intent. Then I attempted to lift our eyes to a further horizon, to look beyond. "It will not always be this way," I said to the tearful group gathered around the small grave. God has promised resurrection and new creation, the utter and total defeat of death, the newness of life that will make all weeping cease and the memory of pain fade away. This is not the end. Finally, in between these two proclamations is a promise: God will be with you every step of the way.

It should not be this way.

It will not always be this way.

God is with you every step of the way.

The hope that Jesus brings does not leave us looking up; it moves us forward and walks with us toward the horizon. The God who made you and the world around you, the God who raised Jesus from the dead, this God will raise you up in Christ by the power of the Holy Spirit. And every minute between now and then, God is with you by His Spirit.

Tie It Together

We look for the resurrection of the dead,
and the life of the world to come.

What does it mean to believe these words?

- It means refusing to believe in the myth of progress.

- It means resisting the temptation to look for an escape.

- It means lifting our eyes to a wider horizon,
  to glimpse the hope of a world made new, of
  resurrected bodies, and of death becoming no more.

What does it mean to live by these words?

- Well, perhaps it means not getting too comfortable
  in the present. Or not being too rattled by things
  not going our way. Even when the darkest moments
  come, we can remind ourselves that it is not over.
  We live in an anxious age. People all around us
  are rattled by politics, by the economy, by wars that
  rage, and more. None of these are to be diminished
  or dismissed. Indeed, hope for a different future is the
  very thing that allows us to say about the present that
  all is *not* well.

What's a Christian, Anyway?

- Resurrection means your worst day won't be your last day. We serve the God who raises the dead (2 Cor. 1:9). It's not over until He says, "It is done."

CHAPTER 12

Amen

What does it mean to confess the Creed? Is it simply to agree to the truth of these words, what some refer to as "mental assent"? Are we checking the box like, "Yeah, I believe that"?

Remember the key word we highlighted at the beginning of this book: *in*. To believe *in* is to trust, to put stock in, to actually have skin in the game.

But the question is, how much? Is this like betting on the score of a game (a practice, by the way, whose ubiquity I loathe)? Is this like guessing the number of marbles in the jar for a take-home prize?

You already know what's coming. To confess the Creed is to place our whole lives—past, present, and eternal future—into the hands of the Father, Son, and Holy Spirit. It is not a personal statement of faith; it is a public act of surrender.

Historian and theologian Phillip Cary put it this way:

To confess *the faith* is to make what we believe into something shared, public, and recognizable, not just a fleeting thought in the heart. The baptismal confession makes us members of Christ's army, and to this day there are places where this confession can get you killed. So confession is more than an expression. It is not just saying what is in our hearts; it is joining a community and sharing in its dangers and tasks as well as its blessings. When we say, "I believe" in our baptism or "we believe" in a Sunday liturgy, we are making a commitment that is a pledge of allegiance, joining us to other believers around the world in the Body of Christ, some of whom are bound to get into trouble for keeping this commitment.[1]

A pledge of allegiance. An enlisting into an army. A joining of a community, sharing its dangers and its blessings. All around the world and all throughout church history, Christians have been painfully aware of the cost—and the joy—of confessing the faith, pledging allegiance to Jesus and His kingdom, and entering a new kind of community of siblings and soldiers.

A COSTLY AMEN

Daniel Nayeri, an Iranian refugee who fled to the United States with his mother and his older sister, shares a hauntingly beautiful account of his mother's (Sima's) conversion to Christianity, a decision that changed the whole course of their family. Sima was a *sayyed* (a title of respect) from the bloodline of the Prophet. But after her daughter, Daniel's sister, had a vision of Jesus and became a Christian at age six while visiting family in the UK, Sima read about Jesus and became a Christian too. And "not just a regular one, who keeps it in their pocket. She fell in love."[2]

Nayeri expounded on the impact of his mother's new faith on her life.

> She wanted everybody to have what she had, to be free, to realize that in other religions you have rules and codes and obligations to follow to earn good things, but all you had to do with Jesus was believe he was the one who died for you.
>
> And she believed . . .
>
> How can you explain why you believe anything? So I just say what my mom says when people ask her. She looks them in the eye with the begging hope that they'll hear her and she says, "Because it's true."
>
> Why else would she believe it?[3]

The word *amen* means "it is true." It's a Hebrew word, one that Jesus Himself used. For a brief while, some second-generation Gentile Christians tried translating it into Greek to use the word *aleuthinos*, but the word was too soft. It meant something like "That's not false," which is similar to our slang phrase "You're not wrong."[4] But it lacked the strong sense of affirmation. They also tried the Greek translation the Old Testament uses, *genoito*. But that was too "wistful" because it meant something more like "would that it were so."[5] They "missed the confident firmness of a present fulfillment." Very quickly, "there was consensus. Soon all were using Hebrew amen."[6]

To finish the Creed with an "Amen" is to say, "It is true. It is so. It is established." But it is to say it with your life, just as Sima did. Nayeri goes on to recount all that his mother gave up, from generational family wealth to her own medical career. But what she gained was far more in her estimation.

> My mom wouldn't have made the trade otherwise. If you believe it's true, that there is a God and He wants you to believe in Him and He sent His Son to die for you— then it has to take over your life. It has to be worth more than everything else, because heaven's waiting on the other side.
>
> That or Sima is insane.
>
> There's no middle. You can't say it's a quirky thing she thinks sometimes, cause she went all the way with it.
>
> If it's not true, she made a giant mistake.
>
> But she doesn't think so.
>
> She had all that wealth, the love of all those people she helped in her clinic. They treated her like a queen. She was a *sayyed*.
>
> And she's poor now.

People spit on her on buses. She's a refugee in places people hate refugees . . . And she'll tell you—it's worth it. Jesus is better.

It's true.[7]

Daniel admitted that it may not make sense to his readers. He made clear that they can disagree and argue and even conclude that his mother is "dead wrong." But no one who says so could make his mother agree with them. He concluded the section of this story this way:

Christ has died. Christ is risen. Christ will come again.

This whole story hinges on it.

Sima—who was such a fierce Muslim that she marched for the Revolution, who studied the Quran the way very few people do—read the Bible and knew in her heart that it was true.[8]

Amen.

THE GREATEST OF THESE

Much of this book has been about faith. The previous chapter was about hope. But the path to credibility, the thing that makes Christianity believable, is *love*.

Love begins with the household of faith. In John's Gospel, Jesus prayed for His disciples to be one. Then He told them how powerful their unity was as a witness to the world. "They will know that you are My disciples by your love for one another" (John 13:35, paraphrase).

John would echo and underscore these words in his own letters to his church plants. "Dear friends, let's love each other, because love is from God, and everyone who loves is born from God and knows God. The person who doesn't love does not know God, because God is love" (1 John 4:7–8).

Jesus said that the world would know that we know God by our love for one another. John said it with perhaps more strength: If we don't love one another, it's clear that we *don't* know God. Why? Because God has made His love clear: This is how the love of God is revealed to us: "God has sent his only Son into the world so that we can live through him. This is love: it is not that we loved God but that he loved us and sent his Son as the sacrifice that deals with our sins" (1 John 4:9–10).

Those who claim to know Jesus ought to know what love looks like: self-giving and sacrificial. That is the kind of love we ought to have for one another.

Tough standard, but it seems John held this conviction deeply. There is an early Christian legend that John as an old man had to be carried out in front of his church and held up so he could speak. The frail apostle of love would look deeply into the people's eyes, wave a finger, and say firmly but with a smile, "Beloved, love one another!" I don't know if the story is true, but you can picture it!

A little more than a century later, Tertullian, a pastor in the North African city of Carthage, wrote that non-Christians would look at Christians and say, "Look . . . how they love one another . . . and how they are ready to die for each other."[9] The love Christians had for each other was remarkable.

I wonder if our neighbors would say that about us. I think about the division in the church in America today. The anger and hostility that seem to be more often about political loyalties than theological commitments. A casual scroller on Christian X (aka Twitter) would wonder what all the outrage is about. Every day, someone new needs to be canceled, someone else is the subject of scorn and digital derision. Some controversy about a sermon or a blog or an Instagram clip is going viral as more and more Christians pile on. Why do we do this? Why do we do this *in public*?

Disagreements matter. And issuing polemics against other Christian teachers is as old as the church itself. Yet there's something about how it happens now. Instead of two respected and credible voices debating issues of substance— like Irenaeus and Origen or Augustine—we have forums that allow anyone and everyone to echo and reinforce, to misjudge and thin-slice, amplifying error and compounding hurt. This brings us back to the way we began this book: recognizing the problem with replacing *credibility* with *popularity*. A person with no training, no commitment to learning, and no devotion to a community can grow their TikTok following and drown out the scholar who has not only logged the hours of study but also has matched it with quiet and faithful service in their local church.

We are not powerless. We can resist voices that are clever

but not credible. We can say with the apostle Paul that though a person speak with tongues of men and angels—though they have a way with words and reels, images and screens—if they have not love, then we should say they have nothing to offer (1 Cor. 13). If they are not committed to understanding the "other" even if they disagree with them, if they are not embedded in the life of a local church, if they refuse to go about the work of challenge and debate in the way of Jesus, then we should not listen to their voices. There is far more at stake than the virality of ideas. The way we love one another is the most powerful sign that we belong to Jesus.

Speaking of our neighbors . . .

HEALING AND HOSPITALITY

If you want to know what the kingdom of God looks like, look at the life of Jesus in the Gospels. The kingdom looks like the King. See what Jesus did. Take notice of what Jesus prioritized. Observe what Jesus was moved by. He taught on the kingdom of God, and then He embodied the kingdom in His miracles and mercy. Of the four Gospels, Luke pays particular attention to the "outsider," the person who maybe didn't grow up as an insider to the covenant community. Luke himself was likely a Gentile, so perhaps he had personal reasons for this perspective. In Luke's biography of Jesus, if you will, he shows Jesus moving toward people on the margins with *healing* and *hospitality*.

Over a dozen stories in Luke's Gospel focus on Jesus

healing someone. A few times, Jesus healed them in order to restore them to the community, whether that be a community in a household or family or the official community centered on the temple. Here are a few examples:

- Jesus cast a demon out of a man who was in the synagogue with the implication that had the man not been freed, he would've been excluded from the synagogue community in just a minute (Luke 4:31–37).
- Jesus healed Simon's mother-in-law, enabling her to take her honored place as host in the household and serve her guests (Luke 4:38–39).
- Jesus cleansed a man with leprosy and instructed him to show himself to the priest so that he could be cleared officially and reintegrated into the community (Luke 5:12–16).
- Jesus healed a man whose friends had lowered him through a roof to get to Jesus. The result was not only awe and praise but the man's ability to go home as a fully functioning member in his household, a place he could not have held in the ancient world as a person with a severe disability (Luke 5:17–26).
- Jesus spoke the word and a centurion's servant was healed. Once again, the physical healing resulted in the release from shame and the restoration of a person's ability to function in their role in society with as much dignity as would have been afforded them in that status (Luke 7:1–10).

- Jesus raised a widow's son from the dead in the town of Nain. Ostensibly, the significance here was that now the widow would be provided for; her son was alive, and thus she would live too (Luke 7:11–17).

Maybe hospitality in the traditional sense is not what comes to mind with these healings. But consider how N. T. Wright put it: "healing inclusivity."[10] Jesus healed in order to include or reintegrate people into their community in particular or into their society in general. Hospitality in the New Testament was not hanging out with your friends. There is a word for that, as my friend and colleague Ben Simonson pointed out to me: *fellowship*. But hospitality was about welcoming the stranger, the outsider. When you put it like that, you see that these healing miracles make a kind of hospitality possible. I'll stop at Luke 7 because a very important story is coming in Luke 10, which we'll address in a moment. First, let's turn to the meals in Luke's Gospel.

The table scenes in Luke are legendary. There are nine, but here are just three:

- Jesus dined with tax collectors and sinners at Levi's house (Luke 5:29–32).
- Jesus ate at a Pharisee's house, where He was visited and anointed by a sinful woman (Luke 7:36–50).
- Jesus took a few loaves of bread and fish and fed at least five thousand people (Luke 9:10–17).

Even the stories Jesus told as He walked through Samaria—a

people who were geographically, culturally, historically, and religiously peripheral to the Jewish community and faith—were often related to the theme of hospitality.

What is it about healing and hospitality? I think Luke told these stories in his Gospel as a way of reminding the early church about how the mission of God takes place in the world. Remember, the book of Acts is Luke's volume 2. The community of Jesus followers will continue to participate in the arriving kingdom of God by the power of the Holy Spirit through their own acts of healing and hospitality. Let me share two quick examples that come early in Acts. In Acts 3:1–10, Peter and John announced healing in Jesus' name to a crippled man outside the temple, who then entered "the temple with them, walking, leaping, and praising God" (Acts 3:8). You see the pattern again? Healing that links to reintegration into a community. You're never going to read these stories the same way again. Then in Acts 4, Luke offered his classic summary paragraphs about the early Christian community:

> The community of believers was one in heart and mind. None of them would say, "This is mine!" about any of their possessions, but held everything in common. The apostles continued to bear powerful witness to the resurrection of the Lord Jesus, and an abundance of grace was at work among them all. There were no needy persons among them. Those who owned properties or houses would sell them, bring the proceeds from the sales, and place them

in the care and under the authority of the apostles. Then it
was distributed to anyone who was in need. (Acts 4:32–35)

Let me put it another way: Love for our neighbor looks
like offering *healing* and *hospitality*. Now we come to a key
moment, a paradigmatic parable in Luke's Gospel. In Luke
10, Jesus was asked who He would define as our neighbor.
He resisted defining a person; He instead outlined a posture.
The posture is one of openness to relationship, a willingness
to *see*—to see someone not like us, someone who is part of a
group we despise—and a willingness to act. But the story of
the good Samaritan is doing more work than we might have
guessed. It is a microcosm, a story that contains within it all
that Luke had internalized about the mission of Jesus in the
wider world. How does the message about the Messiah go
beyond Jewish boundary lines?

The answer is in the parable: through healing and hospitality. The Samaritan binds up the man's wounds, addressing
his pain in a way that brings about healing. And the Samaritan
takes him to an inn and returns to take care of all his expenses.
This is an act of costly hospitality. Augustine, another bishop
in North Africa but from a later century than Tertullian, saw
in the parable a picture of the gospel: Jesus is the despised
outsider far from His home who crossed the chasm to save
us. The oil and the wine are the sacraments of baptism and
the Eucharist—or perhaps the blood of Christ and the Spirit
of God. And the inn is the church, where Jesus sets us to
complete the work of healing through hospitality.

Whether we accept Augustine's allegorical reading or not, the parable is indeed a picture of the gospel. But it is more than that still. It is programmatic for the church; it is a picture of our mission in the world. We are to move toward a world in pain, offering true and full healing, the kind that only Jesus and the Spirit can bring, and generous and sacrificial hospitality.

How can the church today reclaim the way of Jesus and show both healing and hospitality to a broken world? By the stories I hear from pastors all around the world, it's already happening. It looks like food pantries and medical clinics; it looks like service projects and community partnerships across organizations and churches; it looks like helping people find a community of belonging, a safe space to be honest about their longings and fears. One act at a time, the healing and hospitality of Jesus are being embodied in the world.

LET IT BE SAID, LET IT BE DONE

We have come now to the end of our journey together. We began with a massive question: What's a Christian, anyway? We raised it amid the clatter of confusing and contradictory voices. We know what's at stake is our own credibility. We have been losing our way.

Our question set us off on a quest, a journey to find our way home. We went back to the beginning, to the early Christians and the way they understood the faith. We return now to the heart of who God is—Father, Son, and Holy Spirit—and in turn discover what it means to be His people. We fall to our knees and ask God for His grace, for the blood of Jesus to cleanse us, and for the power of the Holy Spirit to fill us. This is what it means to be a Christian.

How now shall we live? How can our ordinary, daily lives become a witness of these things? How can an ancient confession become a living faith? The gospel becomes credible when Christians believe and live like it is true. May our lives be the "amen"; may our lives of love be a resounding amen.

Amen and amen.

Acknowledgments

There are a few people I'd like to thank specifically for helping this book come to life:

I'm grateful to my literary agent and friend, Alex Field, for believing in me and in this project. Your excitement, commitment, and extraordinary talent at framing ideas and finding partners has moved this from passion to possibility.

To my friend Andrew Stoddard—what a blast to work together again. I love your authentic joy and your incredible instincts. Your vision for this project has been a great strength to me personally, and I know it's what sets you apart as a publisher. (Sorry we moved.)

To Daniel Marrs for working so closely with me, line by line, to hit the mark we were aiming for. This

manuscript is tighter, clearer, and stronger than
it would have been without you. Working with a
theologian as an editor is a dream!

To Janene MacIvor for paying attention to each detail,
each endnote and Scripture reference, each phrase
and expression. What I would surely have missed or
messed up, you corrected and cleaned up. What a gift!

To Paul Pastor for taking up the torch toward the end.
You're a poet and a prophet, and your words and
wisdom have helped us tell the story of this book well.

To John Andrade, Lisa Beech, and the entire team at
HarperCollins Christian, Thomas Nelson. Thank you
for bringing your best and for helping the message
reach the people it was written for. You do great work!

I'm grateful, as always, to my family who has made this
book possible.

To my wife, Holly, for your steady and sacrificial love
and for the way you helped me remember the people
I'm writing for. Thank you for always championing
the call we carry.

To our children—Sophia, Norah, Jonas, and Jane. You are
the reason. Period. You are my inspiration, and you
give me hope. May your faith flourish and endure.

To my parents for giving me the faith and for showing
me what a Christian truly is.

Notes

Chapter 1: Finding Our Way Home

1. Songwriter: Matthew James Redman, "The Heart of Worship" lyrics © Capitol CMG Publishing.

2. "Pastors' Credibility Is in Question—Even Among Pastors," Barna Group, February 16, 2022, https://www.barna.com /research/pastors-trustworthy-reliable/.

3. Barna Group, Barna's Spiritually Open Initiative, December 2022.

4. Jonathan Haidt, *The Righteous Mind: Why Good People Are Divided by Politics* (Vintage, 2013).

5. David Zahl, "What the Heart Loves, the Will Chooses and the Mind Justifies: Ashley Null on Thomas Cranmer," *Mockingbird*, January 5, 2011, https://mbird.com/theology /ashley-null-via-thomas-cranmer-on/.

6. Paul Weston, comp., *Lesslie Newbigin: Missionary Theologian: A Reader* (Wm. B. Eerdmans, 2006), 152, Kindle.

7. Weston, *Lesslie Newbigin*, 152.

8. Weston, *Lesslie Newbigin*, 152.

9. Barna Group, Barna's Spiritually Open Initiative, December 2022.

Chapter 2: What's in the Bag?

1. Christian Smith, *Soul Searching: The Religious and Spiritual Lives of American Teenagers* (Oxford University Press, 2005).
2. Jean M. Twenge, *Generations: The Real Differences Between Gen Z, Millennials, Gen X, Boomers, and Silents—and What They Mean for America's Future* (Atria Books, 2023), 300, Kindle.
3. Alexander Schmemann, *For the Life of the World: Sacraments and Orthodoxy* (St. Vladimir's Seminary Press, 2004), 28.
4. Schmemann, *Life of the World*, 28.

Chapter 3: All Together Now

1. Robert Louis Wilken, *The Christians as the Romans Saw Them* (Yale University Press, 2003), 13.
2. Darrell Johnson, *Experiencing the Trinity: Living in the Relationship at the Centre of the Universe* (Canadian Church Leaders Network, 2021), 3.
3. Abbott Kahler, "The Daredevil of Niagara Falls," *Smithsonian* magazine, October 18, 2011, https://www.smithsonianmag.com /history/the-daredevil-of-niagara-falls-110492884/.
4. Kahler, "Daredevil of Niagara Falls."
5. Kahler, "Daredevil of Niagara Falls."
6. Kahler, "Daredevil of Niagara Falls."

Chapter 4: The One and Only

1. Leonard Nimoy, "How Leonard Nimoy's Jewish Roots Inspired the Vulcan Salute," StarTrek.com, July 17, 2021, https://www.startrek.com/news/the-jewish-ritual-that-led -nimoy-to-create-the-vulcan-salute.
2. Michael Bergeisen, "The Neuroscience of Happiness," *Greater Good Magazine*, September 22, 2010, https://greatergood .berkeley.edu/article/item/the_neuroscience_of_happiness.
3. Carmen Joy Imes, *Being God's Image: Why Creation Still Matters* (InterVarsity Press, 2023), 3, Kindle.
4. N. T. Wright, *Into the Heart of Romans: A Deep Dive into Paul's Greatest Letter* (Zondervan Academic, 2023), 167–170.
5. Jean M. Twenge, *Generations: The Real Differences Between Gen Z, Millennials, Gen X, Boomers, and Silents—and What*

They Mean for America's Future (Atria Books, 2023), Kindle edition, 10.
6. Twenge, *Generations*, 392.
7. Twenge, *Generations*, 401.

Chapter 5: The World's True Lord

1. Carmen Joy Imes, *Being God's Image: Why Creation Still Matters* (InterVarsity Press, 2023), 32, Kindle.
2. Aleem Maqbool and Andre Rhoden-Paul, "Coronation: No Drama over Swearing Allegiance, Says Archbishop," BBC, May 2, 2023, https://www.bbc.com/news/uk-65458470.
3. Maqbool and Rhoden-Paul, "Coronation."
4. Maqbool and Rhoden-Paul, "Coronation."
5. Matthew W. Bates, *Gospel Allegiance: What Faith in Jesus Misses for Salvation in Christ* (Brazos Press, 2019), 228.

Chapter 6: The Story Above All Stories

1. C. S. Lewis, "Myth Became Fact," in *God in the Dock: Essays on Theology and Ethics* (William B. Eerdmans, 1970), 58.
2. C. S. Lewis, "Myth Became Fact," in *Essay Collection: Faith, Christianity, and the Church* (HarperCollins, 2001), 141–42.
3. N. T. Wright, *The Day the Revolution Began: Reconsidering the Meaning of Jesus's Resurrection* (HarperCollins, 2016), 84.
4. I am thinking here of Randall Collins's work on *Interactive Ritual Chains* (Princeton University Press, 2004).
5. *The West Wing*, season 2, episode 19, "Bad Moon Rising," written by Aaron Sorkin, directed by Bill Johnson, aired on May 1, 2002.

Chapter 7: New Beginning in the End

1. "About the Eisenhower-Johnson Memorial Tunnel," Colorado Department of Transportation, accessed July 19, 2024, https://www.codot.gov/travel/ejmt.
2. "Eisenhower Memorial Bore," Colorado Department of Transportation, accessed July 19, 2024, https://www.codot.gov/travel/eisenhower-tunnel/eisenhower-memorial-bore.html.

Chapter 8: Giver of Life

1. Michael F. Bird, *Evangelical Theology: A Biblical and Systematic Introduction, 2nd ed.* (Zondervan, 2020), 155.
2. For an excellent book arguing that the doctrine of the Trinity exists in Paul's letters (and thus in his theology), see Wesley Hill's *Paul and the Trinity.*
3. Gordon Fee, *Paul, the Spirit, and the People of God* (Baker Academic, 2023).
4. Gordon Fee, *God's Empowering Presence: The Holy Spirit in the Letters of Paul* (Baker Academic, 2009).
5. My wife, Holly, and I wrote about participating with the Holy Spirit to cultivate fruitfulness intentionally in our book *The Intentional Year: Simple Rhythms for Finding Freedom, Peace, and Purpose.*
6. Haadiza Ogwude, "'The World Has Been Watching': How a Small Service at Asbury Took the Globe by Storm," *Cincinnati Enquirer,* February 27, 2023, https://www.cincinnati.com/story/news/2023/02/27/how-asbury-university-revival-started-globe-by-storm/69937478007/.
7. "The Asbury Outpouring: What Happened at Asbury University?" Asbury University, accessed July 19, 2024, https://www.asbury.edu/outpouring/#schedule.

Chapter 9: An Impossible Dream

1. *Anchorman: The Legend of Ron Burgundy,* directed by Adam McKay, DreamWorks Pictures, 2004.
2. Daryl Van Tongeren, *Humble: Free Yourself from the Traps of a Narcissistic World* (The Experiment, 2022), 11–13.
3. Geri and Peter Scazzero, The Emotionally Healthy Relationships course, week 5. https://www.emotionallyhealthy.org/wp-content/uploads/2019/01/Emotionally-Healthy-Relationships-Workbook-Chapter-1pdf.
4. Gina Zurlo, "Why the Future of the World's Largest Religion Is Female—and African," *Jerusalem Post,* March 27, 2022, https://www.jpost.com/christianworld/article-702461.

Chapter 10: A New Family

1. Robert Louis Wilken, *The First Thousand Years: A Global History of Christianity* (Yale University Press, 2012), 30.
2. Wilken, *First Thousand Years*, 64.
3. Larry W. Hurtado, *Destroyer of the Gods: Early Christian Distinctiveness in the Roman World* (Baylor University Press, 2016), 55.
4. Hurtado, *Destroyer of the Gods*, 90.
5. Hurtado, *Destroyer of the Gods*, 90.
6. Robert Louis Wilken, "The Church as Culture," *First Things*, April 2004, https://www.firstthings.com/article/2004/04/the-church-as-culture.
7. John Dickson, *Bullies and Saints: An Honest Look at the Good and Evil of Christian History* (Zondervan, 2021), 93.
8. John Bodel, quoted in Dickson, *Bullies and Saints*, 93.
9. Hurtado, *Destroyer of the Gods*, 186.
10. Dickson, *Bullies and Saints*, 168.
11. Nijay K. Gupta, *The Story of God Bible Commentary: Galatians* (Zondervan Academic, 2023), 28.
12. Gupta, *Galatians*, 28.

Chapter 11: A More Beautiful Hope

1. Brian E. Daley, *The Hope of the Early Church: A Handbook of Patristic Eschatology* (Cambridge University Press, 1991).
2. Glenn Packiam, *Worship and the World to Come: Exploring Christian Hope in Contemporary Worship* (InterVarsity Press, 2020), 63.
3. Daley, *Hope of the Early Church*, 220–21.
4. Packiam, *Worship and the World*, 68.
5. Nine instead of ten because there was a big numerical gap between numbers nine and ten and not a significant numerical gap between ten, eleven, and twelve.
6. Packiam, *Worship and the World*, 120, table 7.4.
7. James H. Cone, *The Spirituals and the Blues*, 2nd ed. (Orbis Books, 1992), 30.
8. Jayson Casper, "The 50 Countries Where It's Hardest to Follow Jesus in 2024," *Christianity Today*, January 17, 2024,

https://www.christianitytoday.com/news/2024/january
/christian-persecution-2024-countries-open-doors-watch
-list.html.

9. Casper, "50 Countries."

10. "The Paschal Troparion," https://www.oca.org/orthodoxy
/prayers/selected-liturgical-hymns.

11. Packiam, *Worship and the World*, chap. 4.

Chapter 12: Amen

1. Phillip Cary, *The Nicene Creed: An Introduction* (Lexham Press, 2023), 20.

2. Daniel Nayeri, *Everything Sad Is Untrue: (a true story)* (Levine Querido Books, 2020), 195.

3. Nayeri, *Everything Sad Is Untrue*, 195–97.

4. Eugene Peterson, *The Last Word*, 69.

5. Peterson, *The Last Word*.

6. Peterson, *The Last Word*.

7. Peterson, *The Last Word*.

8. Nayeri, *Everything Sad Is Untrue*, 195–97.

9. Alan Kreider, *The Patient Ferment of the Early Church: The Improbable Rise of Christianity in the Roman Empire* (Baker Publishing Group, 2016), 133.

10. N. T. Wright, *The Challenge of Jesus* (InterVarsity Press, 1999), 69.

About the Author

Glenn Packiam is a pastor, author, and practical theologian who serves as the lead pastor of Rockharbor Church in Costa Mesa, California. He earned a doctorate in Theology and Ministry from Durham University (UK) and is a Senior Fellow at Barna Group. He is the author of several books, including *The Resilient Pastor*, *Blessed Broken Given*, and *The Intentional Year*, which he coauthored with his wife, Holly. Glenn, Holly, and their four children live in Orange County, California.